Michael Welch

SLAM DOORS ON THE SOUTHERN

Capital Transport

ISBN 1 85414 296 8

Published by
Capital Transport Publishing
P.O. Box 250
Harrow
HA3 5ZH

Printed by
Thomson Press
Lyon Road
Harrow
HA1 2AG

Front cover photo:
Michael Welch

Back cover photo:
Colour-Rail

Title page:
The views of Victoria station,
separated by 40 years, are
by John Hayward and
Capital Transport

Author's Note

This album is being published to commemorate the end of the SR's slam door electric trains which for decades have been an integral part of everyday life for rail travellers in southern England. Robust and extremely reliable, they have given years of continuous service, but are now being despatched to scrap yards and were all but a thing of the past when this book was published.

The history of this type of stock goes back to 1909 when the LBSCR started electric services using overhead current collection on the South London Line. The LSWR soon followed, but opted for the direct current third rail system which later became standard. The SECR's plans for electrification were postponed by the First World War and implemented by the Southern Railway in 1925. From tentative and humble beginnings the 'Southern' suburban system grew rapidly and became the busiest suburban electric railway system in the world. In the 1930s the 'Southern' pioneered main line electrification, which was progressively extended to cover much of central southern England. After nationalisation the Southern Region of the newly created British Railways replaced much of the decrepit suburban electric stock it had inherited, and then embarked on a further expansion of long-distance electric services. The principal beneficiaries of this policy were the South Eastern Division, with two separate schemes completed in 1959 and 1961, and also the 'South Western' where steam traction was replaced by rather novel push-pull electrics in 1967.

The SR's commuter railway was different from operations on other BR regions, where some managers disparagingly referred to the SR as a 'tramway'. Furthermore, the SR had its own rolling stock design teams and even most of its maintenance facilities were under SR control, so the region had considerable autonomy. The region persisted with traditional tried and tested technology, such as Mk.1 design and construction, incandescent lighting, simple camshaft power control systems, buck-eye couplings and (of course!) slam-doors. Amazingly, the SR was still persevering with Mk.1 stock well into the 1970s, by which time other regions were expecting their first deliveries of Mk.3s! Despite the fact that a vehicle had been fitted with air-conditioning in the early 1960s no further progress was made, so presumably this luxury was not considered to be necessary. The SR rightly wanted to provide a safe and reliable service (not to mention a seat if possible!) for its huge number of peak-hour travellers, and fancy improvements were frowned upon.

In 1972 the last batch of '4 Cig's appeared, and two years later further Bournemouth Line stock went into service and the final series of '4 Vep' units entered traffic. All of these types were based on existing designs, and they were the final Mk.1 slam-door types to enter traffic on the SR. But the SR could not swim against the tide forever and a further development in the early 1970s was the arrival of the 'PEP' stock, the experimental suburban unit with integral construction and sliding doors. Both of these features were almost totally alien to the SR and represented a major break with 'Southern' tradition, and the introduction of this stock marked the beginning of the end for the suburban slam-door fleet at least. Perhaps it is worth noting that in late 1977 the SR fleet totalled 1,252 slam-door units, the only sliding door stock being confined to the Waterloo

Contents

& City and Isle of Wight. In the late 1970s the class 508s, the first suburban sliding door fleet on the SR, was brought into service and all subsequent rolling stock has been of integral construction with automatic doors. The Hidden Report into the terrible crash at Clapham Junction in December 1988 highlighted the relatively poor crash-worthiness of Mk.1 design stock compared to modern units. It is thought that Network SouthEast had plans for the speedy replacement of the remaining slam-door stock, but the privatisation and subsequent break-up of the rail industry ensured these aspirations were deferred for some years.

The first of the new stock ordered since privatisation were the Class 458 'Juniper' units for South West Trains which were ordered in May 1997, followed shortly afterwards by the first batch of class 375s for Connex South Eastern. The first of the latter series, No.375601, was delivered to Ramsgate depot on 20th August 1999. This stock was very much more complex than the existing fleet and staff training, red tape and suchlike delayed the first revenue-earning run until 10th April 2001. In the past new slam door units entered traffic within weeks of release from the works! On South Central the official launch of the new Class 375 'Electrostar' took place on 17th December 2002, but the gloss was knocked off this event when a unit failed, an incident that was widely reported in the press. Many South West Trains services to Bournemouth and Exeter were already provided by modern stock built by BR, and from 21st April 2004 Portsmouth Line passengers started to benefit when the first of the Class 444 'Desiro' units came into service.

South West Trains became the first company to eliminate slam door stock, the final run in public service (apart from the Lymington branch) being the 11.35am Waterloo to Bournemouth on 26th May 2005. Southern ceased scheduled operation on 19th August, but retained a number of units in reserve for a few months. South Eastern Trains was also on course to pension off its last units before the end of the year.

It is hard to believe that the familiar and distinctive sound of train doors being slammed shut, which has been part of railway passengers' daily routine for generations, will no longer be heard. Regrettably, it seems doubtful that many of the units from this era are likely to survive into preservation owing to their requirement for an external power source and unsuitability for operation on a preserved line. In addition, there is the relatively high cost owing to the amount of copper in the traction motors.

My previous album about SR electrics, 'A Southern Electric Album' (Capital Transport, 2003) covered the period up to 1975. In this book I have brought the story right up to date, but have also included a further selection of pictures from the 'green' era which is remembered with affection by so many people. Thanks are due to John Atkinson, Graham Burtenshaw, Chris Evans and David J. Fakes for reading the proof and suggesting a host of corrections to the text. John Atkinson also provided much valuable historical information. Their efforts have greatly improved the finished product. Also, heartfelt thanks go to all of the photographers without whose kind help and co-operation, not to mention foresight in taking the shots in the first place, this album would never have seen the light of day.

4 Lav	4
6 Pul	7
6 Pan	9
5 Bel	10
6 Cor	12
2 Bil	13
2 Hal	17
4 Cor	20
6 TC	23
4 Sub	24
4 EPB	30
4 Com	39
2 EPB	40
2 Hap	45
4 Cap	51
4 Bep	52
4 Tep	55
4 Cep	56
3 Cep	68
4 Big	69
4 Cig	70
8 Mig	84
8 Dig	85
3 Cop	86
4 Cop	87
4 Vep	88
4 Veg	101
8 Vab	102
3 Rep	103
4 Rep	104
6 Rep	106
4 TC	108
5 TCB	110
5 TCT	111

The Maunsell-designed '4 Lav' units were ordered in May 1930 for the Brighton Line electrification. The initial order was for 40 units, but this was later reduced to 33 sets when plans to run a semi-fast service to Worthing were shelved. The underframes for the extra seven had already been constructed and were used instead for other stock. The units weighed 139 tons, were 256ft 9in in length and when delivered seated 70 first and 204 third class passengers. They were originally numbered 1921 to 1953 and Nos. 1921 to 1940 were completed between July and October 1931 with the remainder being built in 1932. Two additional units were constructed in 1940, but the styling, construction and interior finish were based on the '2 Hal' stock. The '4 Lav' fleet was renumbered 2921 to 2953 in 1937 to make way for the '2 Bil' stock which was also later renumbered. The general structure and appearance of these units was typical of Maunsell's designs of that period, the sides being curved apart from the guard's van/cab end of each motor coach which was flat. Unlike contemporary steam stock, however, which had duckets, the '4 Lav' units were equipped with periscopes and were the first 'Southern' emu type to have these as standard equipment. The droplights were wood-framed and a single ventilator louvre was provided on each door. In addition, a ventilator louvre bearing the unit number was positioned on the front of the cab above the headcode panel, but these were later removed. The units were originally fitted with Metropolitan Vickers 275hp 339-type traction motors. They began trials in early 1932 in readiness for the commencement of electric operation from London to Reigate and Three Bridges which occurred from 17th July 1932. The '4 Lav' stock was normally confined to the Brighton Line, but regular workings, usually in the rush hour, also took the units eastwards to Ore and westwards to Littlehampton. Generally, heavy body repairs were undertaken at Lancing, intermediate body repairs at Selhurst and bogie overhauls at Slade Green depot. In this mid-1960s picture the driver of unit No.2924, forming a Victoria to Brighton slow train, looks out for the guard's green flag before restarting from Coulsdon South. The '4 Lav' units were built, of course, long before starting bells were invented, so the driver had to look out at every stop. No.2924 was one of six units that survived into 1969, eventually being withdrawn on 5th April, whilst the bulk of the class had been withdrawn during the previous year following their displacement by '4 Vep's. *Keith Harwood*

4 Lav

The 3.45pm Victoria to Brighton train, formed of '4 Lav' unit No.2944, passes the site of the old Gatwick Airport station on 21st April 1968, just three weeks before its withdrawal. It was scrapped at Chesterfield in October 1968. The remains of the former platforms can clearly be seen in the picture. The original station on this site was called Tinsley Green, which was renamed Gatwick Airport on 1st June 1936 and was closed on 28th May 1958, from which date it was replaced by the 'new' Gatwick Airport station about half a mile northwards. The track layout has changed considerably since this photograph was taken. The curvature of the slow line tracks has been eliminated following the removal of the middle platform and there are now crossovers between the fast and slow lines. This location is officially known once again as Tinsley Green. *Colour-Rail*

Prior to the construction of the Brighton by-pass and widening of the main A23 London to Brighton road, passengers on southbound Brighton Line trains were not really aware that they were approaching the Brighton conurbation until after Patcham tunnel when the rooftops started to appear. Today, however, trains pass beneath two massive road flyovers, which indicate that a large settlement is being approached, before entering the tunnel. These have, alas, obliterated this worthwhile photographic location. This area is known locally as Waterhall, and in this portrait '4 Lav' unit No.2940 is depicted approaching Patcham tunnel with a stopping train from London Bridge to Brighton on 19th March 1967. This train would have stopped at Redhill during its journey, but at the time of writing there is no comparable stopping service and daytime off-peak passengers between Redhill, and many other stations on the line, and Brighton are obliged to change. Unit No.2940 was taken out of traffic in February 1968. *Les Dench*

The unmistakable curves of the station's magnificent roof, the former locomotive works' administration offices, the lofty St. Bartholemew's church and the splendid backdrop of hundreds of chimney pots, not to mention the cluster of hospital buildings on top of the hill, all combine to make Brighton one of the most easily recognisable and best-known railway stations in the country. In this picture, taken on 30th May 1964, Platform Nos.4 and 5 are both occupied by '4 Lav' units, while a red Post Office van can just be discerned by the parcels dock, unloading mails. A green-liveried BRCW Co. Type 3 diesel locomotive stands nearby, perhaps waiting to collect the vans once they have been loaded. Note the neat green 'sausage' signs. A similar shot from the same vantage point today would not be quite so appealing because the works complex was razed to the ground in 1969 and is now a car park, and modern high-rise blocks have sprung up in the background. Note the labelling on the MSB's windows: there is a 'Ladies Only' compartment adjacent to the guards' van whilst only two of the remaining compartments are dedicated for non-smokers. *Colour-Rail*

The '6 Pul' units were built in 1932 for the Brighton Line electrification (apart from two prototype motor coaches built in 1931) and were used originally on the London to Brighton/Worthing services. The '6 Pan' stock was constructed in 1935 when electric services were extended to Eastbourne/Ore and these units had a pantry car rather than a Pullman car. Twenty '6 Pul' and seventeen '6 Pan' units were built and they frequently ran together in service forming a twelve-car train. The motor coaches, which were of all-steel construction, were built by contractors, whilst the trailer vehicles were more conventional for that period, being built using hardwood framing with steel panelling plus timber and canvas roofs. Three of the '6 Pul' units constructed especially to work the 5.0pm London Bridge to Brighton business service were designated '6 Cit', and these provided a higher proportion of first class seats than the standard six-car stock. When new the '6 Pul' units were shown in operating publications as '6 Cor', but when the '6 Pan' stock was introduced this designation was amended to '6 Pul' and the 'Brighton Belle' units, then known as '5 Pul', became '5 Bel'. The Pullman cars were removed from the '6 Pul' units from 4th May 1942 and stored until the end of the war. The units were originally fitted with equalising beam bogies but the riding quality of these deteriorated with the result that rebuilding of the trailer bogies was authorised in 1955. The motor coaches, however, retained their original bogies until withdrawal. The '6 Pul' units rarely strayed away from their routine workings from London to the South Coast, but they were occasionally employed on Royal specials from Portsmouth to Windsor. This photograph was taken on 15th September 1963, the day that the former Caledonian Railway 'Single' No.123 double-headed a Bluebell Railway steam special down the Brighton Line, and shows unit No.3011 passing Wivelsfield at the head of a Victoria to Eastbourne/Ore train. This unit was normally formed with Pullman car *Naomi*. It was one of four '6 Pul' units damaged in an air raid at Brighton on 25th April 1943, but quickly repaired. The Pullman cars were maintained on a different frequency to the other coaches and this sometimes caused units to run as a five-car formation whilst the Pullman was out of traffic. Note that the Pullman vehicle in this shot has been recently repainted, whereas the other coaches are less pristine. *John C. Morgan*

The introduction of '4 Cig'/'4 Big' stock in March 1965 marked the beginning of the end for the Brighton Line six-car units. By the spring of 1966 almost the full complement of new units was available, and with the withdrawal of the final '6 Pul' unit imminent the Locomotive Club of Great Britain organised a farewell tour. Fortunately, one of the last serviceable units was No.3041, one of the former '6 Cit' units that still retained its 1931-built experimental motor coach with straight sided bodywork, so it came as no surprise when this unit was selected for the tour. In this picture No.3041 poses in Platform 7 at Brighton station on 24th April 1966, presumably before leaving on the next stage of its journey to Ore. This tour was anticipated to be the set's last public appearance as a Pullman unit before withdrawal, but it reportedly made one or two later trips in passenger service, probably due to the non-availability of other stock. It should be noted that the motor coach visible in this illustration is a standard vehicle, not the experimental coach. Some coaches from this unit saw further use in '6 Cor' No.3041, which lasted in traffic until December 1968. *Charles Firminger*

6 Pul

Very few photographs of '6 Pul'/'6 Pan' units were submitted for this album, presumably because they were withdrawn when steam traction was still in regular operation. It would be an understatement to say that most photographers were drawn to steam rather than electrics, which were doubtless considered rather boring, and consequently few pictures of electric stock were taken. This shot is the only picture of a '6 Pan' unit offered for publication and although the unit is almost the furthest from the camera (on the extreme left) it can be clearly seen. Note especially the pantry car, which is the third vehicle. The pantry cars, numbered 12501 to 12517, contained a refreshment kitchenette with a counter and five first class compartments. The pantry cars' kitchens were taken out of use from 27th May 1942, but the coaches themselves remained in traffic due to the seating accommodation they provided. The pantry cars became fully operational again from 7th January 1946, but reportedly lost their refreshment facilities permanently in the 1950s. Note the remarkable selection of other stock visible in this portrait which was taken at Eastbourne in June 1965. The unit next to the '6 Pan' is a newly introduced '4 Cig', which is rubbing shoulders with (what appears to be) a '2 Hal'/'2 Bil' formation. The unit in the right background is a '4 Lav'. The stock in the foreground includes '4 EPB' No.5358, which was one of two units of this type specially equipped with express gear ratio motors and B5(S) trailer bogies for use on London Bridge to Eastbourne (and return) peak hour services. The vehicles nearest to the camera (from left to right) belong to a Bulleid loco-hauled set and another '6 Pan' unit. *Roy Hobbs*

The rolling stock orders for the London to Brighton/ Worthing electrification scheme included thirty-eight Pullman cars, twenty-three for use in six-car units whilst the remainder of the vehicles were built as five-car motor sets for use on the 'Southern Belle' all-Pullman service between Victoria and Brighton. They were the first all-electric Pullman trains in the world. Each set consisted of a motor brake third (48 seats), a third parlour car (56 seats), two first class cars (each with a kitchen, pantry and 20 seats) and another motor brake third. The overall length was 335ft and the total weight was 249 tons. The units, which were initially numbered 2051 to 2053, were equipped with heavy self-contained buffers, couplings and gangways to 'Southern' standards. The coach bodies were of all-steel construction and were especially noteworthy due to the high degree of sound insulation. The floors were insulated with compressed cork, whilst the sides and roof had layers of 'Insulwood', which was presumably a proprietary material of the period. The units reportedly cost £35,000 each to build. The title 'Southern Belle' gave way to 'Brighton Belle' in June 1934 and the sets were renumbered 3051 to 3053 in January 1937. In this picture unit No.3053 presents a fine sight as it approaches Merstham on 7th October 1962, a day when trains were diverted via Redhill due to engineering work. Note the decorative Pullman crest on the cab front, this shot being taken in the days before yellow warning panels became mandatory. *Roy Hobbs*

On 20th April 1969 major engineering works took place between East Croydon and Victoria resulting in the 'Brighton Belle' being diverted to London Bridge where unit No.3052 was photographed awaiting departure with the 11.00am service to Brighton. Note that the unit's route indicator stencil remains in use, but this was replaced with a roller blind soon afterwards. In 1968 BR had decided to give the units a heavy overhaul and, most controversially, this included a change from the traditional and attractive Pullman colours to corporate blue and grey, as seen here. The magic word 'Pullman' no longer appeared on the vehicles' exterior, this being replaced by 'Brighton Belle' and it seemed that BR were determined to rob the train of any remaining individuality, which had always been its hallmark. It was a monumental public relations blunder, but BR failed to learn from its mistakes and succeeded in upsetting some of the 'Belle's' famous clientele again when kippers suddenly disappeared from the breakfast menu one morning in 1970! This sparked an outcry and a petition was organised with the result that kippers soon returned to the menu, but not until the press, which took a delight in sniping at BR at every opportunity, had had a field day. *Bryan Rayner*

5 Bel

Fine woodwork above a doorway, incorporating the Pullman coat-of-arms, is seen in this illustration. Car No.91 was a motor coach formed in unit No.3052, and upon withdrawal was one of a number of cars purchased by Allied Breweries. *Colour-Rail*

The plush interior of trailer first kitchen car *Gwen*, which was normally formed in unit No.3053, is seen in this portrait taken on 25th January 1969, shortly before the unit was despatched to Eastleigh Works for overhaul. During this work the first class cars were allocated three-digit numbers, this particular car becoming No.281. These cars, with their comfortable armchairs and remarkably spacious two-a-side seating, represented the last word in luxury. Following overhaul, the seat moquette seen here was replaced with charcoal grey material, whilst the new carpets were mustard colour. After withdrawal *Gwen* was sold to the Horseless Carriage public house, Chingford Hatch, Essex. *Gwen*'s sojourn at Chingford ended some years ago and this car is now part of the V.S.O.E. fleet. *Colour-Rail*

The second class 'Brighton Belle' cars were, naturally, not as roomy as their first class counterparts, nor was the interior décor quite as ornate. But, even so, they were still splendid vehicles by any standard. This picture depicts the interior of trailer second car No.85 at Brighton after arrival formed in the 11.00am from Victoria on 2nd March 1969. It was standard Pullman practice to vary the interior panelling in each car, so every one was different. There was a small illuminated notice in each car stating that it was 'ventilated continuously with clean fresh air'. This may have given unsuspecting travellers the impression that the staff always insisted on the windows being wide open, but actually it referred to the pressure ventilation equipment, the temperature of which was controlled automatically by thermostats. This car, which was previously formed in unit No.3053, is also now owned by V.S.O.E., but is not yet operational. *John Hayward*

When the '6 Pul'/'6 Pan' units were taken out of traffic in the mid-1960s many of the vehicles were given a further lease of life, some trailer coaches being reformed with motor coaches from disbanded '4 Res' units thus creating additional '4 Cor' stock. Some of the '6 Pul'/'6 Pan' units had their Pullman or pantry cars replaced by ordinary trailer coaches, thus becoming '6 Cor' units. These reformed 6-car units did not remain on the Brighton Line, however, but were sent to the South Eastern Division (SED). This division had benefited from a substantial modernisation programme and boasted new trains, improved track layouts to speed-up services and the renovation of some stations. But, despite this investment, the SED was short of main line rolling stock during the rush-hours and also during summer weekends when boat train traffic was heaviest. So, despite the fact that the '6 Cor' units considerably detracted from the SED's modern image, they presumably had to be used because no other stock was available. The '6 Cor's were mainly confined to seaside specials, charter train traffic and peak hour commuter workings. It is recorded that during the 1967 summer timetable, which included additional business services, the units took a full part in rush hour services and on the first day of the new timetable at least four 12-car formations were in use. The units remained in sporadic use during the following year, but all had gone by 1969. In this illustration unit No.3049, accompanied by another unit of the same type, poses at Ramsgate with a Saga Holidays charter train on 1st July 1967. *Terry Phillips*

6 Cor

A Waterloo to Portsmouth stopping train, with '2 Bil' unit No.2008 leading, runs in to Worplesdon station on 10th October 1965. This was one of ten units that were originally intended to be used on semi-fast services from London to Eastbourne. The first to be constructed was No.1890 (renumbered 1900 in January 1936 and 2010 in February 1937) which appeared in February 1935, and the remaining nine units were outshopped shortly afterwards. These units were typical of Maunsell's designs of that time and had door ventilators, cream painted corridor panelling and wooden fillet window fixings. They had Metropolitan Vickers traction motors, unlike the later batches which were equipped with English Electric motors. It should be noted that No.2008's driving trailer coach is a standard '2 Bil' vehicle from unit No.2029, the units having permanently exchanged DTCs as a result of the Ford collision in August 1951. Not surprisingly, these slightly non-standard units were among the first to be condemned when programmed withdrawals commenced and all had gone by the end of 1969. Unit No.2008 was withdrawn on 12th April 1969 and cut-up five months later by Messrs. Armitage of Sheepbridge, near Sheffield. *Ray Soper*

2 Bil

In BR days there was always great camaraderie between railwaymen and in this picture
the driver of this Bognor Regis-bound working, the late Roy Cann, makes a friendly
gesture to the photographer, who was a friend of his and, of course, also a railwayman.
The train is nominally the 11.6am from Victoria to Bognor Regis, but on this particular
day, 20th April 1969, there were engineering works between East Croydon and Victoria
and services were being diverted to London Bridge and the train is seen just after passing
Honor Oak Park. Unit No.2033 entered traffic in October 1936 for the Portsmouth Direct
line electrification and survived until 12th July 1971. It was broken-up by Messrs. A. King
& Son of Wymondham, near Norwich, two months later. Unlike the first ten units, the later
batches of this stock did not have door ventilator louvres and the interior panelling was of
varnished teak rather than cream-painted. They also had larger guards' vans which
reduced the seating capacity in the motor coach, the later series having a coupé third
class compartment with four seats adjacent to the brake van, rather than a full width
compartment seating eight passengers. This reduced the total number of third class seats
to 84, with 24 for first class passengers. *John Scrace*

2 Bil

A number of '2 Bil' units had 'odd' formations as a result of accident damage, one of these being unit No.2133 which is depicted at Three Bridges on 25th May 1970. It was one of three units paired with an all-steel driving trailer composite, the others being Nos. 2069 and 2100. Unit No.2133's DTC (No.12166) was damaged beyond repair in an incident at Guildford in November 1952 whilst the other two units lost their DTCs in the Ford collision of August 1951. Two entirely new vehicles were constructed for Nos. 2069 and 2100 and they re-entered service in 1955. No.2133, however, was formed with coach No.12856 which was nominally a new vehicle. This was built, however, on the underframe of coach No.12133 which was previously part of unit No.2100. The body of this vehicle was destroyed in the Ford accident, but the underframe survived and was stored until 1954 when it was used in the construction of coach No.12856. Unit No.2133 also re-entered traffic in 1955 and lasted until July 1971. Two other '2 Bil' units, Nos.2056 and 2088, ran for some years with '2 Hal' driving trailer coaches. *John Scrace*

The wide crossing gates, controlled from the adjacent signal box, and very solid bracket signal dominate this view of the eastern end of Ford station on 22nd July 1971. Regrettably, this scene has changed beyond recognition since this shot was taken, the gates having been replaced by lifting barriers in 1979, whilst semaphore signals have given way to the all-conquering colour lights. Note the down loop line on the right, also a thing of the past, which was principally used by units working the long-discontinued shuttle service between Littlehampton and Arundel. The train is a Brighton to Portsmouth Harbour semi-fast working led by '2 Bil' unit No.2034, and the formation also includes an all-steel '2 Hal' previously used on the Victoria to Gatwick Airport service, whilst the rear unit appears to be a standard '2 Hal'. No.2034 was one of a large batch of '2 Bil' units built in 1936 for the Portsmouth Direct Line electrification. It was one of the last eight remaining in traffic when this type ceased operation at the end of July 1971, just nine days after this scene was recorded. On 5th August 1951 a dreadful accident occurred at Ford when the 11.17am Brighton to Portsmouth train collided with the rear of the 10.47am Three Bridges to Bognor Regis working. Sadly, there was considerable loss of life, both trains no doubt being well patronised because it was August Bank Holiday. *Bryan Rayner*

This really vintage scene shows a Three Bridges to Bognor Regis train pausing at Horsham in August 1955. The front unit is No.2632, one of 76 similar sets built in 1938/39 for the electrification to Gillingham/Maidstone. These units were somewhat austere when compared to their '2 Bil' predecessors, with bench-type seating in the third class and unattractive painted interiors. The motor coaches comprised of non-corridor compartments, so only passengers travelling in the driving trailer vehicle had access to a lavatory. At the time of this photograph much railway property was still in poor condition following years of post-war stringency as evidenced here by the extremely shabby condition of the platform canopies. One wonders if they had seen a lick of paint since the station was rebuilt in the late-1930s! Note the whitewashed platform edge and brick facing.
David Kelso/Colour-Rail

In this rare view of an electric train on the Mid-Sussex Line (now known as the Arun Valley Line) '2 Hal' unit No.2630 pauses at Christ's Hospital station with a Victoria to Bognor Regis working on 28th June 1969. This unit was new in March 1939 and withdrawn on 4th April 1970: it was scrapped in January 1971 by Messrs. Milton Metals of Cardiff. This station, which was built in 1902 to cater for traffic to the nearby school from which it took its name, boasted an exceptionally attractive frontage and, most interestingly, a track with platforms on both sides like those still in use at Guildford and Norwood Junction today: this is visible on the right of the shot. The signal box, which is just discernible on the left, formerly controlled the junction with the line to Guildford which was closed in 1965. It was a very sad day when BR demolished the buildings in the early 1970s, thus reducing the premises to bus stop mediocrity. *Colour-Rail*

In the early-1950s it was becoming clear that a relief airport to London Heathrow was necessary and in May 1958 Gatwick Airport was opened. The adjacent former Gatwick Racecourse station, which had been rarely used since 1939, was re-built, re-signalled and re-named. The initial service to the 'new' station was provided by half-hourly London to Brighton stopping trains, but from the start of the summer timetable on 9th June 1958 an enhanced service was timetabled. This involved the reorganisation of the half-hourly Three Bridges to Bognor Regis local trains to start at Victoria and routeing them through a new reversible platform at Gatwick Airport station, where a portion was detached and remained in the platform to await attachment to the next up train from Bognor Regis. Unfortunately, it was not possible for the SR to employ its latest stock on this service because it could not work in multiple with the units used on the Bognor trains, so the SR used a small batch of seven '2 Hal' units that had been built in 1948. These units, Nos. 2693-2699, which became universally known as the 'Gatwick Hal's, had all-steel bodies and the profile of post-1945 suburban stock so they were relatively modern and certainly the seating was an improvement on the standard '2 Hal' stock. They also had the advantage of large brake vans for airport passengers' luggage. In this illustration, taken on 9th April 1965, unit No.2696 is seen awaiting the arrival of the portion from Bognor Regis which it would then lead onwards to Victoria. Note the old-fashioned porters' barrow and the appearance of the station that has totally changed after extensive rebuilding. *Terry Phillips*

2 Hal

A Portsmouth Harbour to Brighton stopping train, led by former 'Gatwick Hal' unit No.2694, runs into Portslade & West Hove station on 22nd July 1971: the rear unit is a '2 Bil'. By this date the 'Gatwick Hal' units had been displaced on the airport service by '4 Vep's. Apart from the railway tracks and the roadway, almost everything else in this portrait has since disappeared. The station's awnings were removed many years ago, whilst the semaphore signals and signal box (visible above the first coach) fell victim to a re-signalling scheme in the late-1980s. The goods yard and its associated shed and trackwork have also gone but, almost needless to say, the station premises remain open and probably have the best train service in their history. *Bryan Rayner*

Few SR multiple units could rival the character of the distinctive '4 Cor's. Perhaps the best-remembered characteristic of these units was the manner in which the corridor connections at each end of the unit used to sway crazily from side to side when they were at speed. Due to their long association with the Portsmouth Line, and single windscreen that gave them a 'one-eyed' appearance, the units were known as the 'Nelson' stock. The '4 Cor' units were constructed in two principal batches, Nos. 3101 to 3129 in 1937 for the Portsmouth Line electrification and Nos. 3130 to 3155 in 1938 for the Bognor Regis Line. In addition, three units, Nos. 3156 to 3158, were formed after the Second World War in place of three '4 Res' units, whilst in the mid-1960s a further ten were created using surplus motor coaches from former '4 Res' units plus redundant '6 Pul'/'6 Pan' trailer coaches. This fleet suffered dreadfully during the Second World War, a total of 25 new vehicles being built after the end of hostilities to compensate for losses due to enemy action; many units were severely damaged during air raids in the Portsmouth area. In this evocative picture unit No.3152 is seen at the head of the 12.50pm Waterloo to Portsmouth Harbour train at Woking on 4th October 1964. This unit survived the Second World War unscathed, but was damaged in a derailment on the Quarry Line (near Redhill) on 27th June 1949. *Colour-Rail*

4 Cor

On the Central Section '4 Cor' units were probably most associated with the services down the Mid-Sussex Line (as it was then known) from London to Bognor Regis. In addition they also had duties on the Brighton Line and in this portrait unit No.3112 is seen entering London Bridge station with the empty coaching stock ('e.c.s.' in railwaymen's parlance) of the 5.43pm to Littlehampton via Hove train which had come from the sidings at Streatham Hill depot. This stock always seemed to cope well with snow and ice conditions. Unlike later stock, the '4 Cor's had a through power cable between units which ensured that current from the live rail was available to the traction motors throughout the train even if there was only one collection shoe in contact with the conductor rail. The object in the cab which can be seen through the windscreen is a 'loudaphone', which enabled the driver to speak to the guard and *vice versa. Colour-Rail*

A Victoria to Brighton semi-fast train, routed via Redhill, runs into Burgess Hill station one day during the mid-1960s. The leading unit is No.3114, one of the first series built for the Portsmouth Line. When BR's blue corporate identity colour scheme was introduced some units, of a variety of types, emerged from Eastleigh Works with only a small yellow warning panel on the front end, as seen here. But the painting specification was soon changed to include all-over warning panels which were considered to be more visible to staff working on the permanent way. Alas, the all-over panels were hardly aesthetically attractive but, understandably, safety had to come first. Apart from refurbished platform canopies and improved lighting, plus a new footbridge, this scene has not changed much over the years. The rather cramped station building is still there, perched on the road bridge, and it is still possible to take a picture with an appealing background of mature trees. *John C. Morgan*

Perhaps one of the most remarkable workings during the period covered by this album was that of '4 Cor' unit No.3135 to some of the London Midland Region's North London suburban lines on 8th November 1970. The special, which was organised by the Locomotive Club of Great Britain's Croydon branch, started at Victoria from where it journeyed to Twickenham via Clapham Junction (Windsor Lines). A Class 33 was attached for the short run to Richmond from where unit No.3135 set off unaided into totally uncharted territory, at least for a '4 Cor'! After visiting Broad Street station the '4 Cor' joined the WCML at Camden from where a run was made to Croxley Green via Watford Junction, the former being the limit of d.c. operation. The tour then proceeded to Euston station where the sight (and unmistakable sound!) of one of these units was almost certainly unprecedented. Later the unit worked to Willesden, returning to the SR after reversal at Kensal Green. After regaining SR metals unit No.3135 was apparently booked to run fast from Acton Wells Junction to Windsor – presumably another 'first' for a '4 Cor'. The unit then returned the hopefully satisfied participants to Victoria via Staines, Weybridge and East Putney. One wonders how today's railway authorities would react to the idea of a similar trip using a 'Southern' d.c. unit. *Colour-Rail*

Without a doubt one of the weirdest units seen on SR metals during the period covered by this book was '6 TC' set No.601. This was a rake of miscellaneous trailer vehicles from former Brighton Line six-car units marshalled with two de-motored motor coaches, one from a '4 Res' unit and another from a '4 Buf', and modified for push-pull working. The unit was formed in June 1965 and powered by BRCW Type 3 locomotive (later Class 33) No.D6580, also specially converted for push-pull operation, to evaluate the feasibility of this method of operation which was quite novel at the time. After trials, this combination entered passenger service on the Oxted Line from 17th January 1966. The formation was driving trailer open second, trailer second, trailer composite, two more trailer seconds and another driving trailer open second, giving a total of 30 first and 332 second class seats. The vehicle seen here is No.11154, which was photographed at London Bridge station in the mid-1960s. It previously ran on the Portsmouth Direct Line in '4 Res' unit No.3061 and was later formed in '4 Pul' No.3056 before being commandeered for use in set No.601. It looks most strange without the familiar corridor connection and with a standard trailer bogie, without shoe-gear of course, in place of a motor bogie. In 1967 the unit visited Eastleigh Works, was out-shopped in blue livery, and followed its exploits on the Oxted Line with a spell working between Clapham Junction and Kensington (Olympia). By far its most adventurous working at this time was a trip on the 6.00pm Waterloo to Salisbury on 29th August 1967. In June 1970 it was involved in a collision with a milk tank wagon at Olympia and subsequently remained out of service until withdrawn in October 1971: it was broken-up at Brockenhurst in March 1972. *John C. Morgan*

This absolutely fascinating view of Waterloo station taken in 1957 gives an insight into operations at the terminus at that time. The principal subject is a really ancient '4 Sub' unit, No.4510, which is leaving with an outer suburban train to Horsham. This unit was destined to remain in traffic until December 1959. The coach nearest to the camera is motor brake third No.8860, which was originally part of unit No.1725 formed in 1929. This coach comprised of former a.c. overhead electric driving trailer composite vehicle No.4033, built by the LBSCR at Lancing in 1911, and a former a.c. underframe which had been suitably lengthened. It ran in unit No.4528 until 1956 when that was disbanded and 4510 formed. A passenger peers out of a window, no doubt intrigued by the antics of the photographer. The units on the extreme left are of the '4 Cor'/'4 Res' type, which have presumably formed a working from Portsmouth. In the centre of the picture the front end of a '2 Hal' unit is visible. It is displaying headcode No.12, indicating an Alton Line train. *Marcus Eavis*

A Waterloo to Horsham train, formed of unit No.4512, another of the elderly wooden-bodied '4 Sub' units, enters Clapham Junction in 1958. Both this unit, and No.4510 seen in the previous picture, were formed in 1956/57 from three-car unit Nos. 1702 to 1772. These had originally been built in 1911 to 1924 for LBSCR overhead a.c. services and were converted to d.c. operation in the late 1920s. When this stock was withdrawn in the mid-1950s various coaches deemed to be in reasonable structural condition were reformed into 18 four-car sets numbered 4501 to 4518. Unit No.4512 was formed of coach Nos.8708, 9729, 9739, and 8874 which, apart from coach No.9729, had previously run in unit No.1739. It should be noted that all of the coaches in unit Nos. 4501 to 4518 were of LBSCR origin except for three coach bodies of LSWR design that were mounted on LBSCR underframes. It was expected that these veterans would run only for a further one or two years as a stopgap pending the delivery of new stock, but in the event they ran for longer than had been anticipated. In September 1959 it was reported that many of the units were in very poor condition, and at least one example was apparently running around with holes in its bodyside panelling. No.4512 worked until December 1959 and the last survivors were withdrawn during the following month. *Marcus Eavis*

4 Sub

If an opinion poll were conducted amongst passengers to find the least popular suburban unit design there is no doubt that the first ten '4 Sub' units, Nos. 4101 to 4110, would be very near the top. These units managed to pack no fewer than 468 passengers into their extremely narrow compartments, compared to the 552 seats provided in the 'double decker' stock. In many respects it is a pity that they will always be remembered for their cramped accommodation, because they incorporated several innovations in rolling stock construction. They were the first Eastleigh-built vehicles to have all-welded steel bodysides, but the roof was traditional wood and canvas. Other features introduced with this stock included curved window glass (matching the contour of the bodyside), which was rubber-mounted in steel frames bolted to the body panelling, and the distinctive SR door with a toplight. The units were designed in 1939, but due to the outbreak of the Second World War the appearance of No.4101 was delayed until October 1941, whilst the remainder entered traffic just before the end of hostilities. These units survived until the early 1970s, by which time

they had become the oldest '4 Sub' units in service. In this illustration No.4107 is depicted leaving Wallington with the 3.18pm Victoria to Epsom Downs train on 5th June 1966. Note the points providing access to and from the middle road which was used for reversing purposes, a very unusual arrangement that was still in use (judging by the shiny rail surfaces) at the time of this shot. *Colour-Rail*

The location of this photograph is immediately recognisable as Crystal Palace Low Level station but, alas, the identity of some of the '4 Sub' units depicted here is uncertain. The unit on the extreme left appears to be No.4735, whilst the middle one with the domed cab roof is No.4102. The unit in blue livery with a small yellow panel is No.4117, one of the very few that appeared in this livery. Unfortunately the remaining units are unidentifiable. Could the photographer have asked for a greater choice? This picture shows the older part of the station premises, opened in 1854 as a branch from Sydenham by the LBSCR, but extended towards the capital soon afterwards. This was, of course, built to cater for visitors to the permanent exhibition site which was a hugely popular attraction up to the First World War. The section from Norwood Junction to Crystal Palace opened in 1857, while the link to Beckenham followed a year later. *Colour-Rail*

One of the most fascinating aspects of the '4 Sub' stock concerns the obscure subject of roller blind headcode panels. Needless to say, very few units were fitted as blinds did not become standard equipment until 1951 and the humble '4 Sub's were generally fitted with the stencil plate type of headcode panel. A handful of units was originally equipped with roller blinds, however, and their panels were flush with the cab front panelling, thus giving a clean, uncluttered appearance. Later, other units benefited from this advance in route indication technology (!) and were fitted during heavy overhauls at main works. But, there does not appear to have been a common design which resulted in some units having panels which protruded slightly from the cab panelling. The headcode box fitted to No.4660 broke all of the rules, however, jutting out considerably and making this a unique unit. Here, No.4660 is pictured at Purley whilst forming part of a Coulsdon North to Victoria morning rush-hour train in July 1970.
Bryan Rayner

4 Sub

Few SR outer-suburban terminal stations boast such an impressive background as Windsor and Eton Riverside, where '4 Sub' unit No.4657 is seen posing on 8th May 1980. This unit was completed in January 1950 and lasted in service until July 1983, so it was among the last operational units of its type. The leading unit in the right background is a '2 Hap'. The station seen here is sandwiched between the River Thames, out of sight on the right, and the vast bulk of Windsor Castle which dominates the scene. The station opened on 1st December 1849 and at one time was served by a two-road engine shed. The elegant station was designed by William Tite, well known for his beautifully designed stations on the Hastings Line, and he created a commendably fine building worthy of the historic town it serves. Private waiting rooms were provided for Queen Victoria and the court attendants. *John Atkinson*

For many years the responsibility for the maintenance of the '4 Sub' fleet was shared between Eastleigh Works, which undertook heavy overhauls, Selhurst Paint Shop, which carried out intermediate body repairs and Slade Green Repair Shop, where periodical overhauls of the running gear were undertaken. This meant that the units were often seen at locations well away from their normal sphere of activity. In order to move the stock a network of 'Q' pathways was provided on a daily basis in the timetable. These were pathways for the movement of empty stock which operated 'as required' and a driver and guard were rostered who would take any stock that needed to be moved for maintenance purposes. For example, if a Selhurst-based unit was programmed for attention at Eastleigh Works it would be moved on a 'Q' pathway from there to Wimbledon, which 'connected' with another 'Q' path onwards to Eastleigh. In this picture, taken on a dreary 1st April 1982 at Slade Green, '4 Sub' unit No.4298 is seen presumably heading 'home' to Selhurst after repairs at the repair shop. This is likely to have been its last programmed overhaul, because it was withdrawn, together with all of the remaining '4 Sub' units, in September of the following year. No.4298, which dated from April 1949, achieved a place in railway history when it reportedly formed part of the last diagrammed '4 Sub' working on the South Western Division on 11th July 1983. *Michael Furnell*

In these days of fancy electronic dot matrix route and destination indicators it is, perhaps, difficult to believe that not very long ago the old-fashioned stencil plate type of indicator was still in everyday use on the '4 Sub' stock. Every driving cab was equipped with a box containing a stencil for each number from 0 to 9, which could form every route number worked by electric stock. No.4754 was, presumably, the last unit built with this type of indicator. The roller blind indicators, introduced in the early 1950s, heralded the beginning of the end for the traditional stencil indicator, but they did not finally disappear until the last of the '4 Sub' units was withdrawn. In this shot, taken at Epsom Downs station on 26th August 1983, the driver of unit No.4754 removes the stencil from the front of the unit before 'changing ends', a routine he must have repeated many times. The unit had just arrived with the 3.35pm from Victoria, the other unit being No.4279. This was probably one of the last occasions the driver performed this chore, because the stock was withdrawn a week later. Besides being the only fleet still using a stencil, the '4 Sub' units also needed a tail tamp on the rear because they were generally not fitted with roller blinds. *Chris Evans*

The restored '4 Sub', No.4732, accompanied by preserved '2 Bil' No.2090, traverses comparatively unfamiliar territory as it approaches Southerham Junction, near Lewes, with a special on 7th September 1991. Regrettably, this absolutely magnificent photographic location, which has the South Downs as a backdrop, has since been partially destroyed by a road scheme and industrial development. This was one of a series of workings that took place throughout the summer of that year to mark the 150th anniversary of the Brighton Line, the celebrations culminating a fortnight later in a grand exhibition of both ancient and modern locomotives and rolling stock at Brighton depot. In addition, a programme of special trains was run to and from Victoria. After spending some time in the semi-derelict berthing shed at West Worthing, where it was prone to vandalism, the future of the unique '2 Bil' unit now, thankfully, seems assured. The same, unfortunately, cannot be said of the '4 Sub', which is reportedly in open store at the time of writing in the Coventry area. *Dick Franklin*

Over the years a number of colour views of trains leaving Cannon Street station have been published, but here is something different, a really intriguing illustration dating from 1957 showing the station's interior. The skeletal remains of the station roof cast a pattern of dark shadows across the platforms and retaining wall as passengers clamber aboard '4 EPB' unit No.5258, departure of which will presumably be imminent once the driver has selected a route indication! Note that this unit, which was one of the last of its type to be built, in March 1957, is carrying an 'S' prefix to its unit number. In later years, No.5258 was 'facelifted' as No.5460 and lasted in traffic until February 1994. Perhaps of greater interest is the other

unit, on the left of the picture. It is No.4330, originally a wooden-bodied '3 Sub' constructed for the Eastern Section in 1925, and numbered 1500. In the mid-1940s the unit was augmented to a four-car formation by the inclusion of newly-built all-steel trailer third coach No.10368 and renumbered. No.4330 remained active on the Western Section until displaced by BR Standard '4 EPB' units in late 1961, by which time it was one of the last survivors of its type. No further use could be found for its comparatively new all-steel trailer coach which was one of many of these 'surplus' vehicles cut-up at Newhaven in late 1963. *Colour-Rail*

4 EPB (SR design)

Above Sadly, very few enthusiasts had the foresight to photograph everyday scenes such as that seen here, which were probably considered utterly boring at the time compared to the wonderful shots of steam traction that could be taken. After all, '4 EPB' units would go on forever, wouldn't they? Here, the 2.12pm Charing Cross to Gravesend is depicted leaving Erith on 11th March 1961. It is impossible to read the unit number on the cab front, but the coach number indicates that it is unit No.5048, which dated from November 1953. In January 1962 No.5048 was the subject of trials of yellow warning panels, a full-width panel below cab window level being applied. It was 'facelifted' in October 1986 and lasted until August 1993. Note the neat platform flowerbeds, which would doubtless have been at their best later in the year, and piles of coal in the yard behind the station. *Charles Firminger*

Below Undoubtedly one of the most scenic photographic locations on the South Eastern Division is this view, near the southern entrance to Polhill tunnel, between Orpington and Sevenoaks. In this photograph, on a lovely June evening in 1975, '4 EPB' No.5020 runs downhill towards Dunton Green with a Charing Cross to Sevenoaks outer suburban train. This section of line was electrified in January 1935, when the limit of electric working was extended southwards from Orpington. The stretch from Bickley Junction to Sevenoaks via Swanley was inaugurated at the same time. Sevenoaks remained the limit of electric working for more than 25 years until Phase Two of the Kent Coast electrification scheme was brought into operation in 1961. *Ken Smith*

The route from London to Horsham via Epsom was once used by main line trains from London to Bognor Regis, but these were re-routed to serve Gatwick Airport in 1978 and at the time of writing this line is served only by outer suburban trains. The sizeable and wealthy towns served by the route are not, apparently, considered sufficiently important to justify a through service to the coast. In this portrait, taken on 10th January 1982, '4 EPB' unit No.5011 is seen leaving Ashtead station with a Victoria to Dorking train. One of the drawbacks of slam-door stock are the extremely fierce draughts around the doors, a characteristic especially noticeable in units with a door to each seating bay, as seen here. On a very cold winter's day travel could be quite unpleasant, particularly as the train heating on many units was not, in the author's experience, particularly effective. In any case, heat was quickly dissipated by the doors being repeatedly opened at stations and windows left open. *Dick Franklin*

4 EPB (SR design)

A small number of '4 EPB' units had 'odd' vehicles with an especially interesting history, so the author was delighted when this view of unit No.5005 was submitted. This was one of only four units which ran with a former '4 Sub' nine-compartment trailer second, which had been built as a composite vehicle, rather than the standard ten compartment coach. The other units with these coaches were Nos. 5008, 5115 and 5220. The 'odd' vehicle in unit No.5005 began life in September 1947 as coach No.11454 and it initially ran (as a third class only coach) as part of '4 Sub' unit No.4573. In April 1952 it was reformed into unit No.5005 and re-numbered 15005. It remained in this unit for most of the rest of its career. In April 1988 No.5005 was reformed with another compartment trailer, which replaced its trailer second open coach, and became '4 Com' unit No.5531. It survived in this guise for a further three years being condemned in May 1991 and subsequently scrapped at Messrs. Booths, Rotherham, scrap yard in September of the same year. This picture was taken in October 1983 and shows the unit negotiating the tightly-curved spur from the North Kent line to the Sidcup line, near Slade Green. It was forming an empty stock train from Slade Green depot to London. *Michael Furnell*

The interior of trailer second coach No.15449 of the prototype 'facelifted' '4 EPB' unit No.5263 is seen in this illustration. The unit was working the 12.05pm Holborn Viaduct to London Bridge train on 15th March 1977 and the picture was taken at Wimbledon. This unit was created from '2 Sap' motor coaches and a pair of withdrawn '4 Sub' trailers. The 'facelift' programme started in 1980, the work being carried out at Eastleigh and, until its closure, Horwich Works (near Bolton). In addition to work normally undertaken at a heavy overhaul, the units were converted to all-saloon and fitted with fluorescent lights and public address equipment. Improved draught-proofing was installed around the doors. The first batch of units was fitted with false ceilings, but economies later forced the abandonment of this work and only the first 49 units were done. Few units were 'facelifted' without being reformed, and many were reformed with two compartment trailers immediately prior to the work, both of these being converted to saloons during the 'facelift'. This reformation involved exchanging a trailer with a unit not scheduled for 'facelifting', which thus became all-saloon. Other units, like No.5263, were put together from an assortment of '2 Sap' and '4 Sub' vehicles. It should be noted that there were differences between the production series of 'facelifts' and the prototype unit, so the interior seen here is not entirely typical. *Chris Evans*

Great Britain abounds in magnificent railway photographic locations such as the sea wall
at Teignmouth, County March summit on the incomparable West Highland Line and the
splendid vista of Newcastle Central station from the castle keep. But who would have ever
thought that a multi-storey car park in Lewisham would be a promising location for a
photographic masterpiece? Perhaps the view seen here does not quite have the dramatic
impact of any of the aforementioned, but it certainly portrays the seemingly endless
suburban sprawl that the unremarkable '4 EPB' units served for so long. Here, unit
No.5018 is depicted departing from Lewisham station with the 12.18pm Charing Cross to
Gravesend train on 9th July 1987. *John Scrace*

4 EPB (SR design)

It is, perhaps, rather a pity that, in the author's opinion, the interest of most railway enthusiasts has tended to focus on motive power and infrastructure has been neglected. In this shot Epsom station's magnificent signal box, sitting on a gantry astride two running lines, is surely at least as interesting as the train passing beneath! The unit is '4 EPB' No.5409, which began its career as No.5247. It was 'facelifted' in the early 1980s and renumbered in a new series to denote these partially refurbished units. Following 'facelifting' No.5409 would have been repainted in blue/grey livery, but by the time of this photograph it was in Network SouthEast colours, which were hardly suitable for a unit with so many external doors. Epsom station's signal box, which dated from the rebuilding of the premises in 1929, was an architectural gem. Originally 60 levers were installed, but since May 1969 it had controlled only colour lights, apart from two ground signals. The box gained listed building status and extensive roof repairs were undertaken in 1989. Sadly, this proved to be a bad omen and the signal box was closed in July 1990. Despite the fact that it looks to be in excellent shape in this portrait taken during that month, the box was unceremoniously demolished in March 1992. *Neil Davenport*

4 EPB (SR design)

BR Standard '4 EPB' No.5342 poses at Waterloo station on 12th June 1964. Judging by the unit's exemplary external condition it had just been released from an intermediate body repair at Selhurst which, in those days, included cleaning down the paintwork and a coat of varnish. This repair also included any necessary interior work. No.5342 was one of a batch of 54 units built at Eastleigh Carriage Works in 1960-62 for South Eastern Division services, this particular unit being released for traffic on 22nd February 1960. A further series was constructed during the following year for the South Western Division. These units differed considerably from the more numerous Southern Railway-designed units. In addition to a BR Standard underframe and different body profile the units also had a totally different internal layout. In contrast to the SR-designed stock the motor coaches were of the semi-saloon type, whilst the novel design of the trailer vehicles was noteworthy. Unlike the SR units, which incorporated one compartment vehicle and one saloon coach, the BR-designed stock had a mix of both types of accommodation in each carriage. Unfortunately, blue asbestos insulation was used in this stock and, understandably, BR did not wish to incur the high cost of removal if units did not have a long life expectancy. Consequently some of these units were earmarked for early withdrawal, No.5342 being among the first victims. It was condemned on 6th August 1984 and scrapped by Messrs. Vic Berry Ltd. of Leicester. A number of units was 'facelifted', which also involved removing the blue asbestos, and they survived for much longer.
John Hayward

The photographer would probably have been able to smell the new paint as '4 EPB' No.5601, just ex-works, whisked past Earlsfield station on 30th August 1991. By this date the life expectancy of the '4 EPB' fleet was relatively short, so it is likely that the unit had received only an intermediate repair and its pristine external condition was not completely matched by its interior. No.5601 was originally unit 5320, which entered traffic in March 1960: it lasted until May 1993 and was later scrapped by M.C. Metals. *John Scrace*

The interior of a BR Standard '4 EPB' vehicle. Note the use of attractive varnished wood panelling around the windows and on the seat-ends. Unfortunately, this material was prone to vandalism and is no longer used. Despite the white-painted ceiling the interior of this coach is, perhaps, rather gloomy by today's standards. The dark seat moquette, universally known as 'Trojan', may have worn well, but it did little to brighten up the interior. *Bryan Rayner*

4 EPB (BR design)

Increasing concern about the safety of the travelling public, following various unfortunate incidents of passengers being attacked, prompted a decision to reform the '4 EPB' units. The trailer second compartment coach of one unit would be exchanged with the saloon trailer of another unit, thus creating one all-saloon set, whilst the other unit would have two trailer compartment vehicles. For traffic purposes the latter were known as '4 Com' and renumbered in the 5501 to 5532 series. The compartment carriages were distinguished by a red stripe at cantrail height. The railway authorities decreed that no stock with non-corridor compartments (including some '2 EPB's) was to be used in passenger service after 8pm, and in order to achieve this separate diagrams were introduced which segregated the compartment stock from the standard units. In effect, this meant that the '4 Com' stock was largely confined to peak-hour use only. There were no time restrictions on the use of the all-saloon units. In this photograph No.5524 is seen shunting at Tonbridge on 12th September 1991: the other units are Nos.5519 and '2 EPB' No.6245. Unit No.5524 was originally No.5144, apart from one trailer second coach which came from unit No.5156. The '4 Com' stock was not around for very long, and certainly did not achieve high mileages! No.5524 was formed in April 1988 and withdrawn in September 1991. It was scrapped at the yard of Messrs. Gwent Demolition in South Wales. *John Atkinson*

A scene at Woking station on 18th April 1967 showing SR-designed '2 EPB' unit No.5662 carrying out a shunting move from the up side of the station to the down platforms prior to forming a Woking to Basingstoke shuttle working. Despite the impression given by the route indication, which has already been displayed by the driver, the unit was actually heading away from the camera when this photograph was taken. This shuttle service was provided for a brief period during the last few months prior to full electric working being inaugurated, WR dmu stock being employed for a time before electric units took over. One suspects that regular travellers must have been disappointed by their first taste of electric traction to Basingstoke! This unit was one of 34 sets built at Eastleigh Carriage Works between October 1959 and March 1960 on underframes salvaged from withdrawn '2 Nol' stock. They were unofficially known as '2 Nop' units at one time. They spent the first part of their careers on the Windsor Lines, but in May 1974 were largely ousted from these services by BR Standard '2 Hap' units which were downgraded to second class only and reclassified '2 Sap'. Twenty of the units, including No.5662, were moved to Selhurst, finding employment on the Caterham/Tattenham Corner branches, where 'on train' ticket issuing had been introduced. Those allocated to the SWD could still be seen on the Windsor Lines, in addition to a variety of other routes. In May 1984 No.5662 was 'facelifted' at Eastleigh Works, becoming No.6319. *Terry Phillips*

2 EPB (SR design)

... And here is the former No.5662, photographed 18 years after the previous shot was taken, in its new guise as No.6319. In 1984 it was one of a batch of 15 units fitted with window bars at Stewarts Lane depot for working over the North London Line. The unit is depicted posing in the exotic, and rather unlikely, setting of Dalston Junction station on 6th May 1985 whilst forming the 12.30pm from Richmond to Broad Street train, a service that was discontinued following the closure of the latter station. The units that worked this line were still based at Selhurst depot, running empty to and from Richmond. These duties ceased from 2nd October 1989, when Class 313 stock took over. Like so many units of its type No.6319 finished its days on the South Eastern Division, which proved to be the last refuge for slam-door suburban stock. No.6319 was finally withdrawn on 12th September 1994. *Dick Franklin*

2 EPB (SR design)

Some modern-day travellers on the West Croydon to Wimbledon line, which is now part of the Croydon Tramlink system, would probably be surprised to learn that not many years ago it was a BR suburban backwater with semaphore signalling. They would, perhaps, be even more surprised to hear that it was often operated by electric trains that were exiles from the Newcastle to South Shields line on Tyneside. But it was on that route that unit No.5795, seen here at West Croydon with the 10.44am Wimbledon train on 9th April 1965, began its career. It was one of a series of 15 units built at Eastleigh Carriage Works in 1954/55 for the South Tyneside Line. This self-contained route, with a tiny fleet that was not interchangeable with other stock, must have been expensive to maintain and, at times, an operational nightmare. The units originally incorporated a single first class compartment, until the service became second class only in 1959, and had a larger brake van than their SR counterparts. In 1963 electric traction was abandoned in favour of diesel units and the electric stock found a new home on the SR. It was classified '2 EPB' and numbered in the 5781 to 5795 range. At first the 'new' stock could be found on both the South Eastern and Central divisions, but in 1974 it was all moved to the South Western Division. The units were identified as 'non standard' in the mid-1980s, apparently due to their Mk.1B bogies, and were quickly withdrawn, although some were later converted for departmental service. No.5795 was withdrawn in May 1984 and was one of the few units that never worked again: it was scrapped by Meyer Newman of Snailwell in April 1987. *Terry Phillips*

2 EPB (BR design)

The West Croydon to Wimbledon line mainly traversed a residential area, but at the Croydon end of the line it passed the local gasworks and power station, both of which generated considerable business for the railway. In this picture, taken on a gloomy 20th February 1976, '2 EPB' unit No.5754, forming the 1.30pm West Croydon to Wimbledon train, eases away from Waddon Marsh Halt. This was a double track section of line, but only the right-hand line was electrified, the other track being used solely by freight trains to the numerous industrial installations in the area, so it was really two separate single lines. Trains on this line crossed here (and also at Mitcham Junction) the layout being clearly visible in the picture. The BR Standard '2 EPB' units were built between 1954 and 1958 primarily to allow the introduction of ten-car formations on the South Eastern Division. The stock consisted of a semi-saloon 84-seat motor coach with a 102-seat driving trailer. The latter vehicle comprised a saloon and five compartments. Unit No.5754 was confined to use on this route for a long period, being involved in brake block wear comparison tests with sister unit No.5753. *Michael Furnell*

Friday the 13th May 1983 was an unlucky day for travellers on the line from Woodside to Selsdon which saw its last passenger trains run that day. The line was actually served by services from Elmers End to Sanderstead, both of which stations remained open to passengers because they were served by trains on other routes. The former section of line was recommended for closure in the Beeching Report in 1963, but was reprieved by the Government, an action that clearly met with the wholehearted apathy of most of the local community, because the line remained one of the least-used and most un-remunerative in the London area. In fairness it has to be said that in later years this service (which was in any case infrequent) always seemed the first to be curtailed in the event of staff shortages, so it can scarcely be described as attractive or reliable. Predictably, last day revellers outnumbered *bona fide* passengers on 13th May when '2 EPB' unit No.5746 was photographed at Coombe Road forming an evening train. Ticket offices did a brisk business and probably sold more tickets that day than in the previous few decades, so perhaps the late Doctor (later Lord) Beeching got it right on this one! The last train was the 7.30pm additional return from Sanderstead formed by unit Nos. 5720 and 5209. A stretch of the closed line survives as part of the Croydon tram system. *Les Dench*

2 EPB (BR design)

This scene, which was recorded at the north end of Orpington station on 8th October 1986, shows '2 EPB' No.6407 leading a Tunbridge Wells to Charing Cross train. The other units in the mixed formation are a '4 Cep' and a '4 Vep', while several of the inevitable '4 EPB' units creep into the picture. This was one of a number of these units specially modified to facilitate the issuing/checking of tickets commonly known as 'revenue protection': perhaps 'revenue gathering' would have been a more accurate term. The alterations included cutting a doorway from the driver's vestibule into the passenger saloon in the DTS vehicle and installing a starting bell. In the MSB a door was provided from the guard's brake van into the passenger accommodation. The MSBs seated 79 whilst the DTSs accommodated 90 passengers. The Paddock Wood to Strood line, which had a large number of unstaffed stations and halts, was the principal sphere of activity of this stock, and, perhaps, not the kind of working seen here! These units were sometimes referred to by BR staff as the 'Revpro' stock, but it should be noted that this description was entirely unofficial. Unit No.6407 was formerly No.5716 (later 6216), which dated from September 1954. It was modified for 'revenue protection' duties at Slade Green in March 1986 and remained active until March 1995. It was broken-up by Messrs. Gwent Demolition of Margam, South Wales. *Ken Smith*

2 EPB (BR design)

The 12.40pm from Victoria to Ramsgate arrives at Whitstable & Tankerton on 14th November 1965. On this day trains from London were terminated at Whitstable owing to engineering works between there and Herne Bay. The train is formed of four '2 Hap' units, the leading pair being Bulleid-designed stock, whilst the rear two are BR-pattern units. The front unit is No.5632, which was built at Eastleigh Works in 1958 and remained in service until October 1982. Following withdrawal its motor coach was refurbished for further use in '4 EPB' No.5450, but its driving trailer coach was surplus to requirements and scrapped. During its career this stock could be found on all three SR divisions. For example, in May 1969 fourteen units were transferred to the SWD for use on outer suburban duties, downgraded to 'second class only' and reclassified '2 Sap'. Three years later the entire class of 36 units was concentrated at Brighton depot for use on

'Coastway' services formerly worked by '4 Cor' stock, and this proved to be their last home as composite units. They stayed at Brighton for almost four years, being displaced by BR Standard '2 Hap' stock in April 1976. The fleet then moved to Selhurst where they took over suburban workings from withdrawn '4 Sub' units. A small number of the units was taken out of service during the late-1970s, but the bulk were withdrawn in 1982/83, the motor coaches being earmarked for use in refurbished '4 EPB's, as previously mentioned. The final survivors were Nos. 5604/24/35 which lasted until May 1983. *Terry Phillips*

During the early 1970s the 'Coastway' routes radiating from Brighton were dominated by '2 Hap' unit Nos. 5601 to 5636, these units also having odd workings to London. Unfortunately, there were not quite enough of them to cover the traffic diagrams and allow sufficient 'spare' units for maintenance, so the first two BR Standard units, Nos.6001 and 6002, were also allocated to Brighton. Although both types were classified '2 Hap' they really had very few design features in common. The SR units, for example, had a side corridor in their driving trailer coaches which gave access to three first and four second class compartments, plus the lavatory. There was also a half-compartment adjacent to the driver's vestibule. The BR-pattern stock provided 50 second class seats in a saloon and 19 first class seats in compartments. There was no access provided between the two classes of seating so each had its own toilet, that serving the first class section being reached by a short corridor. The passenger accommodation in the motor coaches of both types was in saloons, however, each having seats for 84 second class passengers in two separate saloons. Externally the units were markedly different in virtually every respect as seen in this illustration of Nos. 5610 and 6002 taken at Brighton on 30th June 1973. *Les Dench*

2 Hap (SR design)

A London Bridge to Coulsdon North suburban working approaches Purley Oaks on 9th August 1982. The leading unit is '2 Sap' (formerly '2 Hap') No.5629, both vehicles being built on old '2 Nol' underframes. The blue/grey livery, which was applied only to a small number of these units, highlights the very distinctive window layout on the corridor side of the driving trailer vehicles. No.5629 entered traffic on the SED in October 1958, but it is likely that it worked on all SR divisions on '2 Hap' diagrams at some time during the 1960s because depot allocation had yet to be introduced. No.5629 spent the early part of the 1970s at Brighton depot for use on coastal services, but was moved to Selhurst in May 1976 for suburban work and downgraded to 'second class only'. It was withdrawn on 14th September 1982 and converted to stores unit No.019, being painted in a version of khaki livery. It lasted until June 1991 and was scrapped by Gwent Demolition at Margam in October 1993. *Bryan Rayner*

2 Sap (SR design)

It is unlikely that many colour photographs of '2 Hap' units in green livery were taken because most railway photographers ignored Kent, where most units operated, after steam traction had finished. So the author was delighted when this picture of unit No.6055 was submitted. The shot is a little confusing because it shows the rear of the 9.40am Ramsgate to Charing Cross train approaching Faversham on the down line during single line working between there and Whitstable on 15th May 1966. The shunt signal is 'off' indicating that the train is about to cross to the up line. Whilst the principal subject is especially interesting, the rest of the scene is equally absorbing. Note the overhead electrification masts in the goods yard. These were installed to enable shunting to be undertaken safely using electric locomotives' pantographs, rather than orthodox current collection from live rails, which would have been a hazard to shunting staff. An electric locomotive is just discernible in the background. Partially obscured by a stanchion is a curious double-armed signal which controlled operations in the yard. On the left is part of the former Faversham motive power depot which was located in the 'vee' formed by the Ramsgate and Dover routes. The depot has no road access for demolition crews and the extremely dilapidated building is a real eyesore: it is still extant at the time of writing. *Terry Phillips*

2 Hap (BR design)

Sunshine and snow are a magical combination for railway photography and considerably enhance this scene which shows an eight-car Victoria to Gillingham train, comprising of two '2 Hap' units plus a '4 EPB', approaching Swanley on New Year's Day 1979. The leading unit is No.6086, one of the Phase One units with Mk.4 motor and trailer bogies. The section of line between Bickley Junction and Swanley was originally built as a double track route, but it was a notorious bottleneck and was converted to quadruple track in 1959 as part of the first stage of the Kent Coast electrification scheme. *Ken Smith*

2 Hap (BR design)

'2 Hap' unit No.6020 was an early recipient of the blue livery as first applied, with small yellow warning panels and white unit numbers. It is seen here leading the 9.36am Charing Cross to Ramsgate train in Tankerton cutting on 12th July 1970. It is likely that No.6020's last repaint would have been in mid-1966 when this short-lived livery was in fashion, but by the date of this picture the unit's blue paintwork was looking very faded and stained with carriage cleaning fluid and appears to have been overdue for further attention. Normally the unit would have received a repaint every 2½ years.
Chris Evans

During the 1970s industrial unrest caused a lot of difficulties for the railways which were frequently affected by problems in other industries. At one time Eastleigh Works was desperately short of upholstery moquette, without which they could not complete major overhauls of rolling stock, and their production line could have come to a grinding halt. The material used in rolling stock has to be strong and durable, and is manufactured to a very high specification, so cannot be bought 'off the shelf' at a local furnishers. An SOS was sent to London Transport who presumably had some surplus RT type bus upholstery available, and this was used in at least nine '2 Hap' units, so if a bus conductor suddenly appeared and asked 'any more fares, please?' he would not have seemed too out of place! Unit No.6168, however, was reportedly re-trimmed using District Line stock material. The interior of an unknown '2 Hap' unit is depicted in this illustration which dates from 18th January 1982.
Bryan Rayner

2 Hap (BR design)

A Charing Cross to Gravesend train via Bexleyheath passes Eltham Park station some time in early 1982. The leading unit is '2 Hap' No.6106, the first of the Kent Coast electrification Phase Two units that were introduced in May 1961: it lasted in service until May 1982. Note the vertical drains fitted to this unit, which were only fitted to a small number of '2 Hap's. Like the stock depicted the station is also a thing of the past, being one of the relatively few London area SR suburban stations to have been closed. Originally opened in July 1908 as ' Shooters Hill and Eltham Park', the station boasted spacious waiting rooms plus long decorative canopies and was one of the most pleasant and well-equipped on the Bexleyheath Line. Its name was shortened in 1927. A new station, simply called 'Eltham', was opened on 17th March 1985 and this superseded both Eltham Well Hall and Eltham Park, both of which were closed. *Michael Furnell*

The western approach to Wimbledon as you may not have seen it before! A strategically placed multi-storey car park provides a splendid view of the 7.28am Portsmouth to Waterloo service approaching Wimbledon on the glorious morning of 29th August 1991. The footbridge in the middle of the picture is a traditional photographic location for railway photographers. The leading unit is '2 Hap' No.4305, which was formerly No.6070, a unit that spent the greater part of its career based at Ramsgate. The renumbering took place in April 1988 following the removal of blue asbestos material. In October 1991 No.4305 became part of '4 Cap' No.3321, this unit being eventually withdrawn for scrap in January 1994. *John Scrace*

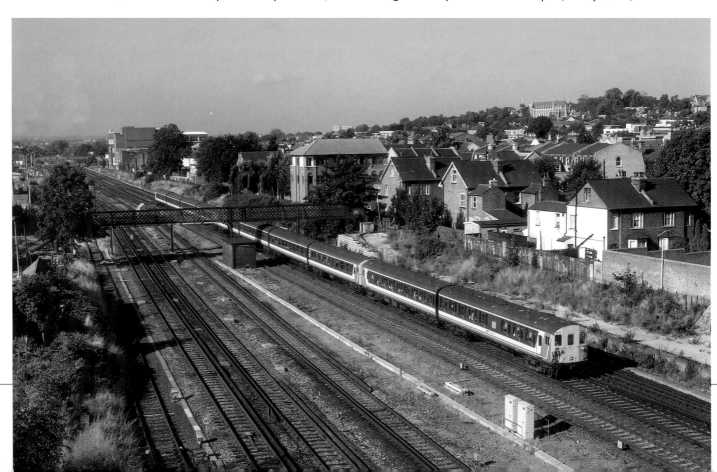

The 1.45pm Victoria to Dartford via Bexleyheath train is seen near Factory Junction on 13th August 1993. This was an additional working provided because of engineering works at London Bridge. The train is formed of '4 Cap' unit No.3305 leading '4 EPB' No.5483. Twenty-four '4 Cap' units were formed in mid-1982 and comprised of two '2 Hap' units permanently coupled with their motor coaches innermost: No.3305 previously ran as unit Nos. 6081 and 6104. Some equipment was removed from the inner cabs and one of the brake vans, the latter being labelled 'luggage'. The units with 1951 electrical equipment were numbered 3201 to 3213 whilst those with 1957 equipment were in the 3301 to 3311 series. All of the units were allocated to Brighton depot for use on 'Coastway' services. In late 1983 three units were transferred to Ramsgate and the remainder followed during the following year. In 1989 the fleet was on the move once again, this time to Gillingham, but the first withdrawals occurred soon afterwards and by the middle of 1991 only 15 units remained. No.3305 lasted until May 1994, by which date it was employed on 'South Eastern' suburban services. Stock in this fleet was rapidly being taken out of service as new 'Networkers' came on stream and the final '4 Cap' in traffic was No.3205 which was condemned in March 1995. It should be noted that a small number of other '4 Cap' units were created in the early 1990s in addition to those mentioned above. *Alex Dasi-Sutton*

In this March 1967 picture of a Victoria to Bognor Regis via Dorking train, unit No.7001 is seen heading a '4 Bep'/ '4 Cep' formation. The precise location is unknown, but the shot is thought to have been taken between Leatherhead and Dorking. This unit was one of a pair of these units introduced in 1956 together with four '4 Cep' units. These were the prototype units and were modelled to a large extent on contemporary Mk.1 locomotive-hauled stock. The cab ends were virtually the same shape as BR Standard Mk.1 coach ends, the driver's controls being to the left of the corridor connection. The electrical equipment (known to BR staff as 1951-type) on these units was different to that employed on the production series, which was the more advanced '1957 equipment'. Internally the prototype units were, once again, different to the standard stock and had narrower seating in the saloons with sprung seats rather than the more comfortable cushions used in the production series. Perhaps the most noticeable characteristic of the prototype units was the use of varnished wood panelling in the coach interiors, apart from the buffet cars, which was in contrast to the formica laminates used in the later batch. An additional point concerns the lack of soundproofing of these units, because the author clearly remembers that the prototype stock was always much nosier than the standard series. *Colour-Rail*

4 Bep

A shortage of photographs of buffet units seems to be an occupational hazard for authors of books about SR electric stock. These were frequently formed in the middle of 12-car trains and, bearing in mind that they were often very small fleets, it is not surprising that pictures are hard to find. In this rare view '4 Bep' unit No.7014 poses at Ramsgate station before departure with a train to Victoria on 24th July 1979. This was one of the Phase Two units built in 1960/61 for the second stage of the Kent Coast electrification scheme, which included the main line from Sevenoaks to Folkestone and Dover. These units had Mk.3B motor bogies and Commonwealth-type trailer bogies plus 1957-type electrical equipment. In the early 1980s unit No.7014 was refurbished at Swindon Works and during the course of this work gained the trailer second from unit No.7186 in place of its buffet vehicle. The latter was also refurbished and became No.69345 in unit No.2305. No.7014 was outshopped as '4 Cep' No.1612 which ended its days working for South West Trains mostly on the Waterloo to Portsmouth route. It survived to become one of the last '4 Cep' units in traffic, being withdrawn in the spring of 2004. *John Atkinson*

A splendidly panoramic view of the 10.50am Waterloo to Portsmouth Harbour train passing the new Covent Garden market between Vauxhall and Queenstown Road, Battersea, on 6th September 1991. The market occupies the site of the former Nine Elms shed, closed in July 1967, which was the last operational steam depot in London. The leading unit is refurbished '4 Bep' No.2303, in Network SouthEast livery, which was, except for the buffet car, originally '4 Cep' No.7208. The latter was one of a small series of these units (Nos.7205 to 7211) actually constructed for the South Western Division, so its conversion to a SWD '4 Bep' was quite appropriate. The buffet car was previously coach No.69018 in unit No.7019 and became No.69343 upon rebuilding. It was originally intended to refurbish all of the buffet cars, but many were uneconomic and it was decided to withdraw buffet facilities entirely from the SED services, and refurbish only seven cars for use on the SWD's Portsmouth Line. The units were numbered 2301 to 2307 and initially mounted on Mk.3B motor bogies and Commonwealth trailers, which were later exchanged for Mk.6 motor and B5(S) trailer bogies. The units seated 134 second class passengers (including 24 in the buffet) and 24 first class. There were also 6 unclassed seats in the buffet car. In September 2002 No.2303 exchanged its buffet car for a '4 Cep' trailer second open (TSO), was renumbered 2313 and reclassified '4 Cep'. *John Scrace*

This was the view from East Croydon signal box at approximately 3.06pm on 17th July 1984 as the 2.50pm Victoria to Hastings train approached East Croydon station. The leading unit is '4 Tep' No.2703, one of four units formed to cover for Brighton-based '4 Big' units which were spending protracted periods away at main works for asbestos stripping. These units, which were relatively short-lived, were made up of three coaches of a refurbished '4 Cep' unit plus an unrefurbished '4 Bep' buffet car. The number series was 2701 to 2704 and the units were based at Brighton. Unit No.2703 was previously '4 Cep' No.1560 (*ex-* No.7152), the buffet car being formerly part of No.7021. This hybrid unit entered service on 22nd December 1983 and ran until March 1986, when it was disbanded to allow No.1560 to be reformed for use on the Hastings Line. There was no further use for the buffet car, which was consigned to a scrap yard. *John Scrace*

A Victoria to Dover Marine (later Western Docks) boat train, formed of three '4 Cep' units plus a motor luggage van on the rear, approaches Petts Wood station on a summer's day in 1962. The front unit is No.7120 which, many years later, was refurbished at Swindon Works, becoming No.1543. The tracks in the foreground on the left are those of the Charing Cross to Tonbridge main line, which the train is about to join. Unit No.7120 was a Phase One unit which was built in November 1958 for the electrification from London to Dover and Ramsgate via Chatham: these units had Mk.4 motor and trailer bogies. The double-glazed windows fitted to this stock had a design fault which prompted much public criticism of BR. Unfortunately, the windows were not, apparently, completely air tight with the result that condensation occurred between the panes and some windows became opaque. In the worst cases an inch or two of water would collect at the bottom of the window prompting suggestions from some humorous passengers that BR might like to start breeding goldfish, so that travellers would at least have something interesting to look at on the way to work! A cure for this problem proved elusive with the result that many of the inner panes were removed and the stock remained single-glazed until refurbishment took place. *John Snell*

4 Cep

The 2.10pm Ramsgate to Victoria train leaves Whitstable & Tankerton on 31st March 1968. The leading unit is '4 Cep' No.7106 in blue livery with a small yellow warning panel: note that the unit numbers on the cab front are painted white. When depot allocation of rolling stock was introduced on the SR in the early-1970s, No.7106 was permanently based at Brighton, where the '4 Cep' fleet was not intensively used and consequently the units were not overhauled as frequently as their Ramsgate-based counterparts. When the refurbishment programme was under way Brighton-based units could be deferred owing to their low mileage and, in the event, No.7106 was the final unrefurbished '4 Cep' to run, lasting until July 1983. It became No.1561 (apart from one coach which went to unit No.1562) which survived as a '4 Cep' until November 1998, when its TSO vehicle was removed. It was reclassified '3 Cep', renumbered 1102, and lasted in service until condemned at the end of March 2003. *Terry Phillips*

A Portsmouth Harbour to Brighton semi-fast train, formed of '4 Cep' No.7102, enters Hove station on 10th July 1971. This unit was one of the four prototype '4 Cep' units introduced in 1956 and used at first on the Central Section. These units could be distinguished from the production series by conduit along the roofs, plus bodywork and internal styling which were very similar to the Mk.1 stock that was being built at that time. No.7102 came to an untimely end on 22nd October 1975 when the two coaches nearest to the camera in this picture (Nos.61036 and 70038) were engulfed by fire while the unit was berthed in Preston Park sidings. Unlike other '4 Cep' units that have been damaged by fire, it seems that in this case arsonists were not to blame, the conflagration apparently being caused by an electrical fault. Unfortunately, the sidings at Preston Park are not accessible by road, and there must have been some delay before firemen could reach the blaze, which partially gutted the vehicles mentioned. A motor coach of unit No.7107 was also damaged and the two units were temporarily reformed in order to create one serviceable unit. No.7102's undamaged motor coach later found a new lease of life in departmental service, while the trailer vehicle was refurbished as part of unit No.1501. *Bryan Rayner*

Photographed just two days after entering traffic, the prototype refurbished '4 Cep' unit, No.7153, is seen drawing to a halt at Bromley South station with the 12.14pm Dover Marine to Victoria train on 11th February 1976. During the extensive rebuild the layout of the unit was radically altered, the guard's vans being replaced by small second class saloons whilst the trailer second vehicle was converted into a saloon. There was only one guard's van in the 'new' unit, this being positioned in the trailer composite. Commonwealth trailer bogies replaced the Mk.4 bogies, but the original motor bogies were retained in the same position, at the outermost ends of the unit. In redesigned units the guard now enjoyed a smoother ride in a trailer coach, but it is questionable whether the passengers seated directly above a motor bogie benefited. *Chris Evans*

The interior of one of unit No.7153's motor coaches is seen in this shot which was taken at Dover Priory on 18th June 1977. Several design alterations were made before further units were refurbished, most notably the change to hopper window ventilators, but also to the ceiling panels and interior décor. Many people considered the prototype unit to be aesthetically very pleasing, with a better ambiance than the later more austere units, and it is a pity that it was thought necessary to change the original design so radically. *Chris Evans*

About 20 of the first refurbished '4 Cep' units were given six-figure numbers, but soon after the refurbishment programme started this policy was changed in favour of four-figure numbers which had always been standard SR practice. Six-figure numbers would have made the daily operation of the railway unnecessarily complicated for operating and maintenance staff, who are continually quoting unit numbers to each other, and they doubtless breathed a sigh of relief when common sense prevailed. In this portrait '4 Cep' No.411517 runs into Borough Green & Wrotham station with a Victoria to Ashford train on 13th March 1982. In the late 1990s this unit moved from the Kent Coast lines (by that time operated by Connex) to South West Trains (SWT). It remained with SWT until the spring of 2004 when it returned to Kent with other SWT '4 Cep' units to replace some Ramsgate-based units which were in particularly poor condition. No.1517 worked out its mileage prior to withdrawal which occurred on 13th August 2004, so the unit only worked for South Eastern Trains (who had replaced Connex) for about four months. *Bryan Rayner*

The 'wrong kind of snow' may have been falling when this shot of a diverted Charing Cross to Hastings train was taken at Haywards Heath on 13th January 1987, but it does not seem to be troubling the two '4 Cep' units forming the train, as they speed through on the down fast line. Note the cloud of steam which is probably the result of snow being blown in through the motors' cooling grilles. The identity of the train is not known, but the number of the snow-encrusted rear unit is 1522. The ill-considered remark about the snow made by a BR spokesman was derided by the media, and has gone down in history with other memorable phrases such as 'peace in our time' and 'the pound in your pocket'. The author well remembers that the fine, powdery, dry snow seen in this picture was indeed the 'wrong kind' at least from the SR's point of view. It played havoc with units' traction motors, motor generator sets and grids and resulted in a record number of units being out of service with electrical defects. So, the BR spokesman's clumsy excuse for the passengers' plight was actually largely correct and it was the media who got it wrong! *Tim Baker*

The cliffs between Dover and Folkestone are one of the best-known landmarks in the south of England. Most travellers on cross-channel ferries from the continent no doubt have enduring memories of the white cliffs of Dover, which were for many their first sight of England, but nowadays most passengers obtain their first glance as their Eurostar train bursts out of the Channel tunnel. Its opening has dramatically altered travel patterns between Great Britain and the continent, and the 1.55pm Dover Western Docks to Victoria boat train, seen here threading Folkestone Warren on 15th July 1990, is now, like so many of the ferries, a thing of the past. The train is formed of three units in 'Jaffa Cake' livery, the leading unit being No.1617. The outstanding section of line between Dover and Folkestone is reported to be one of the most expensive to maintain on the national system due to geological problems. *Dick Franklin*

First impressions, it is said, are always important, so one dreads to think how first-time visitors to Great Britain, who had just disembarked from a ferry at Folkestone Harbour, reacted to the appalling eyesore of the derelict coaches, visible on the left, berthed near the former Folkestone East station. Surely, BR could have found a more suitable storage site, where they would have been less conspicuous? At least the 8-car train of empty stock, formed of two '4 Cep' units with No.1588 leading, is in much more respectable condition, but the graffiti mars its appearance somewhat! The driver would have been keeping a hand on the brake handle as the train descended the 1 in 30 gradient towards Folkestone Harbour station. At the time of writing the branch is used only by the V.S.O.E. Pullman train, whose patrons transfer to coaches at the harbour station. So, the Channel tunnel has largely rendered the Folkestone Harbour branch redundant and it seems unlikely that it will survive for much longer. *Dick Franklin*

A Victoria to Dover Western Docks boat train, led by '4 Cep' unit No.1590, makes a fine sight as it passes through Denmark Hill station on 13th August 1990. The station buildings were severely damaged by fire some years before this shot was taken, but presumably enjoyed listed buildings status and a decision was made to restore them to their former glory. Part of the station has found a new lease of life as a public house. Certainly the buildings provide a striking backdrop to this picture. No.1590 was not fortunate enough to be listed, but at least it had an extremely good innings. It was previously No.7155, one of the early Phase Two units, and became one of the so-called 'magnificent seven' South Eastern Trains '4 Cep' units that survived for more than a year after the rest of the fleet had been condemned. It was eventually withdrawn in early May 2004 following the arrival of a batch of SWT '4 Cep's at Ramsgate. *John Scrace*

The 1.46pm Dover Priory to Charing Cross train, formed of '4 Cep' No.1593, speeds through Folkestone Warren on 5th November 2003: the western entrance to Abbotscliff tunnel is visible in the background. This was a beautifully clear day and very warm for the time of year but, even on a perfect day, the author saw only one other person during a three-hour spell of photography at this location, so it can be quite a lonely spot. Unit No.1593 was another of Ramsgate depot's 'magnificent seven' '4 Cep' units and in early 2004 it received a considerable amount of attention to improve its bedraggled appearance. Its yellow ends were repainted, windows bars fitted and new headrests fitted to many seats in the standard class passenger accommodation, all of which suggested that the unit would remain in traffic for a considerable period. Alas, it was not to be, and No.1593 was withdrawn, together with sister unit No.1594, on 26th March and was hauled to Immingham for scrapping on 6th April. *Author*

4 Cep

The 1.36pm Ramsgate to Charing Cross via Canterbury West service sets off from Ramsgate on 23rd March 2004, formed of green-liveried '4 Cep' No.1592. It should be said that this livery was hardly appropriate for a refurbished '4 Cep' unit, the doors and windows of which were arranged differently to the original units but, even so, it added a splash of colour to an otherwise rather boring and monotonous railway scene. No.1592 was repainted at Ramsgate depot in July 2001, so its external condition was much smarter than some of its sister units, most of which still bore faded Network SouthEast livery. Despite the fact that No.1592's livery was not historically correct for a refurbished unit, it soon gained celebrity status and was known as the 'Green Goddess' to some operating staff. One of the unit's first assignments following repainting was its appearance at the 'Hastings 150' celebrations at the beginning of September 2001. Many enthusiasts probably thought that such a high profile unit would survive until the end of slam-door stock on the 'South Eastern', and it must have come as a shock to many when it was included in the cull of the surviving Ramsgate-based '4 Cep' units in May 2004. *Author*

The interior of coach No.61778 of '4 Cep' No.1592, which was photographed at Canterbury West on 26th July 2002. When the unit was repainted green in 2001 it appears that it was purely a 'minimum expenditure' cosmetic operation and no work was done on the interior, which retained standard Network SouthEast upholstery. In the author's view the refurbishing of this stock was totally misguided, and resulted in these units being much less comfortable for the travelling public. The replacement of the original, cosy seats, with their soft cushions and side head restraints was bad enough, but to add to the passengers' misery hopper windows, which cause draughts of incredible ferocity, were also fitted. The old coach interiors, with their variety of formica panelling, were much more welcoming than the very bright panels used in the refurbished stock, the interiors of which had the ambience of a hospital operating theatre. At least all of the 'new' units had Commonwealth bogies and double glazing, so the changes were not all bad! Well, not quite. *Colin Scott-Morton*

In SR days the vast majority of '4 Cep' units were based on the South Eastern Division, whilst around a dozen were allocated to Brighton and latterly used mostly on peak hour services. This stock occasionally helped out on the South Western Division at times of rolling stock shortages, but it was never a regular performer. The SED started withdrawing these units as long ago as 1993, and in 1996 a small batch was temporarily moved to the 'South Western', which was by this time operated by South West Trains, a Stagecoach PLC company. The Ramsgate '4 Ceps' were owned by the Porterbrook train leasing company and when Stagecoach bought this company in 1997 it made good business sense for them to acquire a fleet of these units. During that year Stagecoach returned some of their '4 Vep's to their lessor and replaced them with '4 Cep' units. The SWT fleet of '4 Cep' units eventually numbered twenty-nine, plus seven '4 Bep's, which gave a total of 36 former Kent Coast units. They worked far and wide across the SWT network, including long distance services such as Waterloo to Wareham, and proved to be very capable performers despite their advancing age. Rather embarrassingly for their operators, this stock was exceedingly reliable, much more so than the modern units. Obviously, the '4 Cep' units could not run forever (well, not quite!) and when the introduction of new Class 450s commenced in 2003 the '4 Cep' units, being by far the oldest in SWT service, were first in the firing line for withdrawal. Before the demise of the standard units at the end of April 2004 a batch was moved to South Eastern Trains, so only four, Nos. 1533/34/65/73, remained with SWT: in addition there was, of course, a small fleet of 'Greyhound' units. The final working is thought to have been that of No.1534 on the 10.38am Waterloo to Portsmouth Harbour on 30th April: on arrival at Portsmouth it was removed to the scrap line at Fratton depot. In this picture No.1533 is seen at Godalming leading the 2.53pm Waterloo to Portsmouth Harbour train on 22nd April 2004. *Author*

4 Cep

The 5.05pm Winchester to Southampton Central stopping train, formed of '4 Cep' No.1573, approaches the site of Bevois Park goods yard, between St. Denys and Southampton Central, on 14th April 2004. The stretch of water on the left is part of the River Itchen. This unit was originally No.7170 and, as previously mentioned, survived to become one of SWT's last operational standard '4 Cep' units. It left Fratton depot, on its final journey to Immingham for breaking-up, on 12th May accompanied by No.1581. Note the excellent external condition of this unit that was only a week or so away from withdrawal when this picture was taken. No doubt this was matched by a spotless interior which, in the author's opinion, is typical of SWT's commendably high standard of carriage cleaning. *Author*

After the previous picture showing an immaculate South West Trains '4 Cep', this illustration depicts the absolutely diabolical and squalid condition of South Eastern Trains' (SET) unit No.1615, which does not appear to have visited Eastleigh Works for many years. It is pictured working the 3.30pm Charing Cross to Ashford train at Sevenoaks on 4th May 2004. The flaking roof paint may not have mattered too much to the passengers, but the appalling state of the unit's paintwork would not have escaped their attention, nor its filthy exterior. Note especially the red upsweep around the cab window that was presumably the target of graffiti 'artists' at some stage. Presumably the red paint 'disappeared' when the graffiti was being removed by an over-zealous carriage cleaner, and nobody seems to have bothered to retouch it. Another of this unit's horrors was a fair number of completely opaque 'pink' sidelights (windows), such as the third one from the camera in this shot, no doubt a result of prolonged condensation. The author well remembers one particular sidelight in which about three inches of rainwater had collected between the panes, and this ebbed and flowed with the motion of the carriage, providing free entertainment for the passengers. Similar problems were experienced with this stock when it was first introduced more than 45 years ago, so presumably it was proving difficult to find a cure! The internal state of No.1615 was also woefully neglected, with missing seat head bolsters, grubby floors and stained upholstery. Perhaps SET gave a refund to passengers unfortunate enough to travel on this mobile scrapheap! Mercifully, No.1615 was put out of its misery when it was withdrawn two days after this shot was taken, and left Ramsgate on 11th May *en route* to Immingham for scrap. *Author*

4 Cep

The 4.26pm Ashford International to Charing Cross train approaches Otford on 4th May 2004. The train was travelling slowly at this point due to a severe permanent speed restriction around a very tight curve at the approach to Otford station, this being an ideal location to photograph the train in very poor light on a dreary afternoon. The front unit is the unique No.1602, the only '4 Cep' to receive Connex livery, and another of the 'magnificent seven' units that remained in traffic long after the other 'South Eastern' units had been withdrawn. Its livery was applied during a visit to Eastleigh Works for repair following an incident near London Bridge in January 1999. This was scheduled to be No.1602's final day in traffic and it was expected to be taken out of service on arrival at Ramsgate later in the day. In the event it survived for a couple more days and exactly a week after this shot was taken it was noted being hauled through Wandsworth Road station, accompanied by Nos.1562 and 1615, *en route* for breaking-up at Immingham. *Author*

During early 2004 the withdrawal of 'slam-door' units really started to gather pace so the transfer of a batch of South West Trains' '4 Cep's to Ramsgate in the spring was a surprising development. Those involved were standard unit Nos. 1517/35/39/50/55/71/78 and 'Greyhounds' 1697/98/99. At least the maintenance staff at Ramsgate would not have needed a familiarisation course! SWT markings and the orange bodyside stripe were painted out before the units entered service. Ramsgate's own remaining '4 Cep' units which, as previously mentioned, were in extremely run-down condition, were withdrawn immediately the new arrivals began work. Despite their comparatively smart condition the units were not destined to last for long and all had been taken out of traffic by mid-September. Unit No.1535, seen here leaving Broadstairs with the 3.04pm Margate to Charing Cross train on 22nd May, lasted at Ramsgate for less than four months, arriving on 17th March and being withdrawn on 6th July. This unit, formerly '4 Bep' No.7006, incorporated former Mk.1 second open coach No.3992, which was built as long ago as 1954, and this was one of the oldest coaches still in everyday use on the national system. *Author*

In mid-1993 six '4 Cep' vehicles had their TSO vehicles permanently removed for use mainly on stopping trains along the Paddock Wood to Strood 'Medway Valley Line', where their improved acceleration from the many station stops was a great asset. The 'new' units were, almost needless to say, known as '3 Cep's. Four more conversions were planned for the Redhill to Tonbridge line, but never carried out and in June 1994 all of the units were withdrawn. A further batch of five units was converted in October 1998 for the Maidstone East line and also for some services to Tunbridge Wells. Initially they retained their own numbers, but were later renumbered 1101 to 1105 in a separate series. Thirteen more units were converted to '3 Cep's in May 1999 and became 1106 to 1118. In early 2003 the Connex management decided that the fitting of the Train Protection Warning System equipment (TPWS) to the '3 Cep's could not be justified in view of their limited life expectancy, and when this became mandatory from 31st March 2003 they were withdrawn. During their last week in traffic they were observed on front-line work, such as the 10.35am Victoria to Ramsgate train, which is seen here on the four-track section at Newington on 27th March. The front unit is No.1102, formerly No.1561, which lost its TSO in November 1998. Interestingly, No.1561 was previously unit No.7106, the last unrefurbished '4 Cep', which is depicted elsewhere in this album. *Colin Scott-Morton*

3 Cep

In this really evocative shot, taken on 29th March 1968, the 3.45pm Brighton to Victoria train is seen leaving Patcham tunnel formed of unidentified '4 Big' and '4 Cep' units, both of which are in green livery. The poor condition of the '4 Big's paintwork, which has been stained by carriage cleaning fluid, will be noted, but the rear unit appears to be in far better shape. As previously remarked in this volume, this view has since been radically altered by a massive road scheme. The '4 Big' units were introduced in 1965/66 for use in conjunction with the '4 Cig' stock on Brighton Line services where they ousted the pre-war '6 Pul'/'6 Pan' units. The units consisted of a DTC (24 first class seats and 28 second), a buffet car, a non-driving second class motor coach (56 seats) and another DTC (18 first and 36 second class seats). This gave a total of 42 first and 120 second class seats. The buffet cars contained a bar, small kitchen area, with electric cooking and refrigeration equipment, and 40 additional second class seats at tables. The new

stock provided 44 more second class seats in a 12-car train than the pre-war units, though the number of first class seats was slightly less. It should be noted that these figures do not include seats in Pullman, pantry or buffet cars. Much of the interior décor and seating design of this stock was based on the Kent Coast express units, the last of which was completed a year before the first of the new 'Brighton' stock was outshopped. The front ends were re-styled, however, with rounded bodyside corners and with brake hoses plus jumper cables mounted in recesses. The use of an intermediate motor coach was a major break with previous 'Southern' practice as were the B5(S) pattern trailer bogies. *Terry Phillips*

The 9.51am Victoria to Hastings train, with '4 Big' unit No.2206 leading, accelerates away from Clapham Junction on 22nd July 1991. This unit was one of ten built in 1970 for the Portsmouth Direct Line, first entering traffic as No.7054, but becoming 2206 in a re-numbering scheme in about 1985. These units had the same internal layout as the first series of '4 Big' stock built five years earlier for the Brighton Line, but benefited from Mk.6 motor bogies, which gave a better ride than the bogies fitted to the Brighton stock. The '4 Big's only lasted for about 12 years on the Portsmouth Line, being displaced by re-furbished '4 Bep' units in the early 1980s. The fleet was then transferred to Brighton *en masse* and most remained there as buffet units until those facilities were withdrawn by Connex in 1997. The very last '4 Big' in service with a buffet in use ran on Christmas Eve of that year: perhaps that was Connex's idea of a Christmas treat for passengers! The units later had their buffet cars removed for scrap and were converted to '3 Cop's, No.2206 eventually becoming No.1404. The buffet car depicted here was exported to Bahrain for use as a static restaurant by an oil company, a far cry indeed from Wandsworth Common! *John Scrace*

In the early 1960s services from London to the Sussex Coast were still operated by the '6 Pul'/'6 Pan' stock which was built in 1932/33 when the Brighton Line electrification was inaugurated. In late 1964 the first of the 'Brighton Line Replacement Stock' (to quote its official title) appeared and the prototype unit, No.7301, was proudly exhibited at Waterloo for the benefit of the SR hierarchy on 6th November 1964. One of the 'new' Reading to Tonbridge line 3R 'Tadpole' units was also displayed on the same day. New SR stock had traditionally been constructed at Eastleigh Carriage Works, usually on frames laid at either Lancing or Ashford works, but the new Brighton Line units, classified '4 Cig', were built at York. This represented a major break with 'Southern' practice and furthermore the design of the stock was quite unlike anything the SR had seen before. Rather than have two motor coaches at the outer ends of the units, the '4 Cig's had an intermediate non-driving power car with both bogies powered and the electrical equipment concentrated in that vehicle. Curiously, the first class seating was located at the outer ends of the driving trailer coaches and this arrangement meant that first class passengers had to walk through the second class accommodation to reach the toilet. Some of them apparently found this rather demeaning and letters from irate commuters criticising the stock's layout appeared in the press. These units were built just before BR adopted its blue/grey corporate image colour scheme and were out-shopped in standard SR green livery, so at least one SR custom was retained, even if only for a fairly brief period until their first repaint. In this mid-1960s view an Eastbourne to Victoria train, with unit No.7315 leading, passes Wivelsfield. *John C. Morgan*

4 Cig

A view of Clapham Junction station on 4th March 1967 showing the back of an unidentified Victoria-bound train, the rear unit of which is '4 Cig' No.7333. The career of this unit was abruptly cut short due to its involvement in the Sweet Hill collision outside Brighton on 19th December 1978. On that day it was forming the rear portion of the 9.50pm Victoria to Brighton train which was halted by a signal north of Patcham tunnel, this being caused by the traction current being switched off at Brighton station due to a person on the track. The following 9.40pm Victoria-Littlehampton, which was running out of course due to an earlier incident in the London area, ran into the back of the 9.50pm train at full speed. The signal at the rear of the 9.50pm was not showing an aspect due to a component failure, and this defect was the major cause of the collision, but the other incidents were also contributory factors. Regrettably, three people lost their lives in the crash, including the driver of the 9.40pm train. The damage to rolling stock was substantial, largely due to the fact that unit No.7333 had come to a stop in the very confined space of a cutting adjacent to Sweet Hill bridge and one coach was actually under the bridge. The rear three vehicles of unit No.7333 were totally destroyed and the remains were broken-up on site, but the fourth coach, DTC No.76108, survived. This coach, which is the nearest to the camera in this illustration, was used as a 'spare' vehicle for some years and was in many different units at various times. In March 1991 it was permanently formed in No.1221 after that unit had lost its own DTC in a derailment at Ash Vale. No.1221 was facelifted in April 1992, renumbered 1870, and transferred to Ramsgate where it stayed until withdrawn in June 2004. *Colour-Rail*

There are many attractive railway routes in the south of England, one of the author's favourites being the Mid-Sussex Line (now called the 'Arun Valley Line') particularly south of Pulborough. The landscape between there and Arundel is especially appealing, with excellent views of the meandering River Arun, the South Downs and finally, at the approach to Arundel, the stunning sight of Arundel Castle which dominates the town. Here, a train from Bognor Regis/Portsmouth to Victoria, led by '4 Cig' unit No.7406, approaches the southern portal of North Stoke tunnel, just south of Amberley on 16th August 1980. The tunnel takes its name from a nearby hamlet. *John Atkinson*

Unit No.1702 positively gleams as it enters Clapham Junction station at the front of a West Worthing to Victoria train on 1st September 1985. The unit had just been released from Eastleigh Works following an overhaul and repainting in the popular, but extremely short-lived, 'Jaffa Cake' livery and this was its first day back in traffic. One can almost smell that new paint! No.1702 was formerly unit No.7326 and later became one of the first units of its type to be withdrawn. Only eleven '4 Cig' units were painted in these colours and when Network SouthEast came into being it was decreed that the 'odd' units in this livery would have to be repainted, because they would not fit in with their 'image'. Surely, the average passenger would not care if the trains were painted black, so long as they were clean and punctual, but to the image-obsessed NSE management the livery was, apparently, all-important and the repainting was duly carried out at Selhurst. *John Atkinson*

The castellated northern portal of Clayton tunnel is one of the best-known features of the Brighton Line, perhaps because it is clearly visible from the Burgess Hill to Brighton main road (just visible on the left) which crosses the railway nearby. Rail passengers obtain only a fleeting glimpse as their train enters or leaves the tunnel. The justification for this remarkable – and no doubt rather costly – structure is unclear, but the most popular theory is that a castle represents strength and security and the castellation would reassure early travellers about to plunge into the cavernous $1\frac{1}{4}$ miles-long bore. It is not known what was done to boost the confidence of northbound travellers, because the southern entrance to the tunnel is not decorated in any way! In the mid-1990s Railtrack, the now defunct rail infrastructure company, refurbished the structure and the cottage above which is a private residence. In this pleasing view the 4.11pm Littlehampton to Victoria via Hove, with '4 Cig' No.1734 leading, is depicted leaving the tunnel on 1st June 1996. *Colin Scott-Morton*

A roadbridge to the west of Hastings station provides a splendid vista of Victorian villas which almost encircle the station's environs. In this picture '4 Cig' No.1712 leaves Hastings on the first stage of its journey to Eastbourne with the 1.15pm to Victoria on 14th August 1994. This unit first saw the light of day as No.7304, one of the earliest of these units to be constructed in late 1964. Almost forty years later it was one of the last of the Phase One units still in service, so had certainly stood the all-important test of time very well. Incredibly, the original station here consisted of one through platform for 'South Eastern' trains and a bay for 'Brighton' services. Two extra bay platforms were later added to relieve congestion, but it was 1931 when the premises were rebuilt in their present form. A three-road engine shed used to stand on what is now part of the down platform visible on the left of the picture. *John Scrace*

A Bournemouth to Waterloo stopping train, formed of '4 Cig' unit No.1882, slows for its stop at Parkstone station one day in September 1995. The unit is in Network SouthEast colours. Built as unit No.7415 it was renumbered 1215 in the mid-1980s and became No.1882 after being 'facelifted'. The unit appears to have spent its entire career on the 'South Western' and, at various times, has been based at Eastleigh, Fratton and East Wimbledon depots. In the distance a few of Poole Harbour's dockside cranes are visible, whilst just discernible is the tree-covered Brownsea Island and, on the far horizon, the Purbeck Hills. *Author*

Most rail travellers know that it is always better to avoid using the railway at weekends, if at all possible, due to the disruption frequently caused by engineering operations. From the railway enthusiast's point of view, however, this vital work does have its compensations when trains are diverted on to an unusual route. One such occasion was on 12th April 1997 when the main Waterloo to Portsmouth route was apparently partially blocked by engineering work and services were being diverted via Epsom and Effingham Junction. In this picture an unidentified 8-car Portsmouth Harbour-bound train, led by '4 Cig' unit No.1310, is seen near Epsom Common. The rear unit is presumably a '4 Bep'. Note that No.1310 is bearing the early style of South West Trains livery, which is basically Network SouthEast colours but with the initials 'SWT', in the centre of each coach, and branding 'A Stagecoach Company'. This unit, which has an interesting history, started its career (apart from the TSO vehicle) as '4 Big' No.7055, which was later renumbered 2207. In October 1988 it was 'facelifted' and reformed with redundant buffet car No.69315, which originally ran in Brighton Line '4 Big' No.7045. The latter coach was converted to a TSO vehicle and renumbered 71926, the newly formed '4 Cig' unit becoming 1823. In May 1990 electrical modifications were carried out on this unit in order to enhance its acceleration and it was renumbered into a new series to indicate these so-called 'Greyhound' units. It should be noted that the maximum speed of these units stayed at 90mph, and even this was academic on such a notoriously curve-infested route as the Portsmouth Direct Line where this stock was largely employed. *Neil Davenport*

No doubt much to the relief of many customers, in 2001 Connex had their franchise for the South Central lines terminated, the Go-Ahead group taking over. They introduced a pleasing new livery for rolling stock and quite a few '4 Cig' units that were due for shops were painted in the new colours. Little work was, however, undertaken on the interiors which was, perhaps, understandable in view of the planned replacement of these units. Strangely, only one South Central '4 Vep' unit, No.3514, was repainted in the new livery: presumably that was the only one due for a repaint. The unit seen here at Barnham is No.1908 which was working the 10.39am Chichester to Victoria train on 1st March 2002. It began life as No.7321 and was later 'facelifted' becoming No.1732. In the early 1990s a number of spare Mk.6 motor bogies became available following the withdrawal of the '6 Rep' units and No.1732's existing Mk.4s were exchanged for a pair of Mk.6 bogies. The unit was then renumbered 1908 in a new series intended to distinguish Phase One units with different motor bogies. *John Scrace*

The line between Redbridge and Millbrook stations, in the Southampton suburbs, skirts an area of parkland bordered with tall trees and in this picture the photographer has used this attractive backdrop to good advantage. The train in view is the 1.10pm from Poole to Waterloo, formed of '4 Cig' unit No.1320, and this shot was taken on 16th April 2002. This is a particularly busy section of line which carries passenger trains on both the Bournemouth and Romsey routes, in addition to relatively heavy freight traffic. Note the distinctive South West Trains livery, which became standard on this type of stock. *John Scrace*

Today's railway photographers have to contend with a whole range of hazards from dense lineside vegetation to unsightly radio masts plus intrusive pallisade fencing, and these have resulted in many locations being ruined. Some rather beautiful rural photographic spots have remained totally untouched, however, and in this view taken in September 2002 a Victoria to Bognor Regis train is depicted between Pulborough and Amberley in the Arun Valley. The 8-car formation is led by '4 Cig' unit No.1869 whilst the rear unit is in white livery. Part of the ancient Amberley castle is visible on the right of the picture while the slopes of the tree-covered North Downs can be seen in the distance. *Author*

4 Cig

In the author's view the early batch of '4 Cig'/'4 Big' stock built between 1964 and 1966 for the Brighton Line had seating almost as cosy as the average fireside armchair. Deep sprung cushions, large armrests and seatbacks with wings to rest your head .... there was no doubt that the comfort of passengers was high on the designer's list of priorities. This interior picture of coach No.70713 (unit 1706) was taken at Eastbourne on 2nd August 2002. This luxurious style of seating was also originally used in the production series '4 Cep'/'4 Bep' units. In the author's opinion much of the seating in today's trains compares unfavourably with the standard depicted here, although it must be admitted that improvements have occurred in other areas. Unit No.1706 was among the first batch of '4 Cig' withdrawals which occurred on 1st November 2002, but the coach depicted in this picture was later reformed into a '3 Cop' unit. *Colin Scott-Morton*

A Victoria to Bognor Regis/Portsmouth train passes Stoats Nest Junction, between Purley and Coulsdon, on 30th July 2003: the Redhill line appears to be blocked by engineering works. Note the leading unit, '4 Cig' No.1864, the first coach of which, DTC No.76812, is fitted with hopper windows. This non-standard equipment was installed during an extensive rebuild at Slade Green depot following a serious fire which occurred at Cooksbridge on 8th November 1985. The conflagration is thought to have been started deliberately. Presumably Slade Green had no sidelights with sliding ventilator windows available, so they used '4 Cep'-style hopper windows which would have been readily available from Ramsgate depot. This distinctive unit, which entered traffic in June 1971, was previously No.7391, later 1291. It was 'facelifted' in September 1991, when its identity was changed to No.1864. *Chris Evans*

The lovely old signal box, vintage hand-operated gates and painted advertisement on the wall of an adjacent building conjure a delightful image of a bygone era in this picture taken at Chartham in January 2004. The signal box, which dates from 1888, has been reduced in status to a gate box following the introduction of colour light signalling on the Ashford to Minster route, but the crossing keeper is still kept extremely busy running across the road in all weathers (and directions!) to open or close the gates. The building on the right is presumably a former Fremlins-owned public house. The '4 Cig', No.1701, is also of considerable interest being, at the time of the photograph, one of three Phase One units in white livery operating with 'South Eastern'. The other units were Nos.1742 and 1748. It was previously No.7312 and was 'facelifted' in July 1985 when renumbering occurred. It ran with Connex South Central until September 1997 when it was taken 'off lease' and despatched to Shoeburyness. In January 1998 it was rescued from there and sent to Eastleigh Works for a running gear overhaul, repaint and the removal of its electric parking brake, with which all Phase One units were originally equipped. In April 1998 it returned to service, but this time at Ramsgate depot, where it remained until withdrawal in June 2004. It left Ramsgate for the last time on 21st July *en route* for breaking-up in South Wales accompanied by sister unit No.1742. *Author*

4 Cig

This location may not immediately be recognised by many readers, but the strip of waste ground on the right adjacent to the running lines was sometimes used in the past to stable carriages awaiting entry to a nearby works, so this provides a good clue. This spot is in fact a few hundred yards east of Lancing station and the picture shows '4 Cig' unit No.1837 forming a Brighton to Littlehampton train on 29th January 2004, a rare winter's day without even a hint of cloud in the sky. Prior to the closure of the carriage works here in May 1965, Lancing was very much a 'railway town', but one wonders how many of the current occupants of the houses visible in this shot work on the railway. *Author*

4 Cig

The Portsmouth Direct Line has a reputation among today's railway photographers as an extremely difficult route to photograph due to the lack of suitable locations, and very close proximity of vegetation to the running lines for much of its length. But at least the route does have this magnificent stretch between Rowlands Castle and Petersfield where it passes the South Downs, and where, moreover, the relative lack of lineside growth gives uninterrupted views. Here, on 7th February 2004, a northbound train formed of two unidentified '4 Cig' units reflects the late afternoon sunshine as it heads past Idsworth, whose famous old church, situated in the middle of a field, is visible in the background. This picture was taken from the slopes of Chalton Down which rises to a height of 476ft. and offers a splendid panorama of the railway and surrounding landscape. *Author*

4 Cig

Unit No.1870 may appear at first sight to be just another '4 Cig' in Connex livery, but actually it was a unique unit with an eventful history. It was built as No.7421 (later No.1221) and spent the first part of its career at various depots on the SWD. On 29th August 1990 it was derailed at Ash Vale and DTC No.76771 sustained sufficient damage to warrant its temporary withdrawal for long-term repairs, this coach eventually being permanently formed with No.1208. In the meantime No.1221 was returned to service in March 1991 with spare vehicle No.76108, formerly part of No.7333, three coaches of which were destroyed in the accident at Patcham (near Brighton) in December 1978. This formation became permanent, and in April 1992 No.1221 was 'facelifted', renumbered 1870 and entered traffic on the 'South Eastern' based at Ramsgate. Apart from the fact that it ran with a Phase One driving trailer coach, this unit also became the only 'South Eastern' '4 Cig' to be repainted into Connex colours. In this illustration it is seen leading the 8.55am Charing Cross to Ramsgate/Dover train away from Paddock Wood on 9th February 2004. This working could be relied upon to produce an interesting selection of multi-coloured stock and on this day was formed of No.1878 in Network SouthEast livery, in the middle, and No.1748 in white on the rear, in addition to No.1870. The latter spent a long period on a back road at Ramsgate during the spring of 2004, but surprisingly re-entered service until final withdrawal came in June of that year. *Author*

4 Cig

The 4.35pm Margate to Charing Cross train, formed of '4 Cig' unit No.1840, passes underneath the impressive elevated signal box at Canterbury West on 30th March 2004. There were formerly two signal boxes at this location, both of which were replaced on 1st January 1928 by the structure seen here. This city is particularly rewarding to enthusiasts with a special interest in signalling, because Canterbury East station also boasts a signal box perched on a gantry, but that is a more modest affair and does not span the tracks. No.1840 was previously unit No.7374 (later 1274) which spent much of its life at Brighton depot. It was withdrawn in the spring of 2004 and was removed from Hither Green to Immingham for scrapping on 3rd June. It had been booked to go direct from Ramsgate to Immingham, but was stabled at Hither Green for a few days after a locomotive failure. *Author*

4 Cig

An afternoon Waterloo to Portsmouth Harbour via Eastleigh train, with '4 Cig' unit No.1309 leading, leaves Winchester on a damp 2nd July 2004. The unit on the rear appears to be a '4 Vep'. No.1309 was put into traffic on 30th July 1970 as No.7350, being included in the 'Portsmouth Line' batch of twenty '4 Cig' units, Nos.7337 to 7356, which were initially based at Fratton. It was renumbered 1250 in August 1987 and became 1822 when 'facelifted', and released in Network SouthEast colours, on 26th July 1988. It was later modified as a 'Greyhound' unit and was again renumbered, becoming 1309 in April 1990. *Author*

During the '4 Bep' refurbishment programme the SR was short of buffet units, so two temporary buffet units were put together using '4 Cig' units and two restaurant miniature buffet coaches. The units were numbered 2601 and 2602 and allocated to Fratton depot. The first-mentioned was made-up of No.7401, three coaches of No.7402 and an RMB vehicle, No.1872. The units, known as '8 Mig', entered service in May 1983 and offered 312 second class seats, 84 first and 44 seats in the unclassed buffet vehicle. It was not possible to heat the buffet coach, so the units only worked during the summer of 1983, being withdrawn from 3rd October when the heating season began. They were usually confined to the Portsmouth Direct Line and, in this exceptionally rare shot, No.2601 is seen here near Vauxhall forming the 4.53pm Portsmouth Harbour to Waterloo on 21st July 1983.
Chris Evans

A close-up picture of unit No.2601 showing its strange formation with locomotive-hauled buffet car No.1872 formed between two '4 Cig' driving trailer coaches. The buffet coach had been specially converted in the early 1970s to permit multiple unit operation and this ingenious short-term formation at least ensured that early morning commuters were able to enjoy their usual cup of coffee on the way into London. This picture was taken at Woking on 27th August 1983.
John Atkinson

In early 1993 it was decided to form a small, dedicated fleet of four units to operate certain London to Brighton fast services which were being especially marketed as the 'Capital Coast Express'. The units were formed of a '4 Big' and '4 Cig' permanently coupled together and were known as '8 Dig' units. The unit numbers were carried on the outer ends only. The buckeye coupling release chains were removed from the intermediate driving trailer coaches to prevent inadvertent dividing of the units. The units were put together using stock recently released from Eastleigh Works, and in order to present a positive image to passengers using this prestigious service some modest internal enhancements were made. These included the fitting of curtains in the standard class accommodation (in some units), moquette panelling around the trinket trays and improved gangway curtains. Seats were fitted with clips to enable the fastening of special 'Capital Coast Express' antimacassars. Externally, logos were applied to some coaches and the train's name appeared on each driving trailer vehicle. There were three diagrams for the dedicated trains, whilst a fourth operated on ordinary Brighton Line services, the idea being that it could quickly provide cover in the event of a failure. The units operated with other stock during the peaks and, curiously, there was a diagram that took one of the units to Bognor Regis where it berthed overnight. The units were ousted in January 1997 when the 'Connex Express' service was inaugurated using refurbished Class 319s. In this portrait unit No.2002 is seen approaching its destination with the 12.08pm Victoria to Brighton service on 27th October 1994. Note the external embellishments. *John Scrace*

8 Dig

85

The 12.00 noon Seaford to Littlehampton train, formed of '3 Cop' unit No.1409, nears Durrington-on-Sea station on 15th May 1998. The roof of the West Worthing carriage berthing shed is just visible in the distance beyond the footbridge. This unit was originally '4 Big' No.7057, which later became No.2209. It was renumbered 1409 in September 1997 and continued to run as a four-car unit before going to Eastleigh Works for overhaul in about January 1998, whence it emerged without its buffet car as a three-car unit. During its time at Eastleigh numerous internal modifications were undertaken including the replacement of the first/standard class compartments with four-a-side standard class open-plan seating. Other changes included the partial removal of glass partitions, some toilets being taken permanently out of use, and the installation of a window in the partition between the guard's compartment and the adjoining passenger accommodation to enable the guard to watch out for trouble-makers. If Her Majesty's Prison Service had ever wanted to transfer convicts between Lewes and Ford by rail this unit would have been absolutely ideal! No.1409 was named *Operation Perseus* at Eastbourne on 18th August 1998 to mark the launch of a police operation to combat vandalism, disorderly behaviour and fraudulent travel on the East Coastway route from Brighton. No doubt passengers who later travelled on this rather humble unit were impressed with its name, proudly displayed on the motor coach, but one wonders how many realised its significance. The buffet car that previously ran with No.7057 is preserved at the time of writing at Aysgarth station in Wensleydale, North Yorkshire. A total of eleven '4 Big' units were converted to '3 Cop's, all for use on the 'Coastway' routes from Brighton. *John Scrace*

3 Cop

When the withdrawal of 'slam-door' stock started to gather pace it became clear that the various operating companies would seek to minimise expenditure on the old stock. After the displacement of the '3 Cop' units on the coastal routes from Brighton by new stock some units in good condition, that were not due for major attention, became available for use on other routes and were augmented to four-car formations by the addition of a trailer second vehicle from a withdrawn '4 Cig'. This presumably allowed the withdrawal of other four-car units due for programmed heavy maintenance. In this illustration former '3 Cop' No.1406 is depicted at St. Denys on 14th April 2004, having just negotiated the very tight curve through the station with the 2.17pm train from Victoria to Southampton. This unit was made up to four vehicles by the inclusion of a 'spare' trailer second from unit No.1750. This train was advertised to convey first class accommodation which was not provided: presumably the availability of such accommodation was not high on South Central's priorities! When these augmented units were disposed of the former '4 Cig' TSOs, which were owned by a different rolling stock company to the rest of the unit, had to be separated from the other vehicles. This was done to ensure that the Porterbrook-owned coaches went to Immingham for breaking-up and the vehicles owned by Angel Trains were sent to Caerwent, South Wales! *Author*

An unidentified westbound train, formed of '4 Vep' unit No.7708 in all-over blue livery, is seen heading away from Woking in the summer of 1967. This was one of 20 high-density units built in 1967 for the Bournemouth Line electrification and this batch had minor differences from the later series. Firstly, the motor coaches and trailer open vehicles were built at Derby Carriage Works whilst the driving trailers were constructed at York. Note the different condition of the DTCs' roof paint compared to the other vehicles. All other units of this type were built entirely at York Carriage Works. The driving trailers were also amongst the last coaches constructed for the SR to incorporate blue asbestos insulation. In addition, the livery of this batch of units was different to later units. They were outshopped with small yellow warning panels, whereas the remainder had all-over front-end panels, and unit Nos.7701 to 7711 had painted window frames unlike the rest that had unpainted aluminium frames. In later years No.7708 was 'facelifted', becoming No.3408. *Colour-Rail*

4 Vep

West Worthing is one of those exceptionally interesting stations due to the fact that it has an unusual track layout, with a 'middle road' reversing siding sandwiched between the running lines. This feature is clearly visible in this shot of '4 Vep' unit No.7785 entering the station with a Portsmouth Harbour to Brighton slow train in 1987, just before the replacement of semaphore signals on the West Coast Line. The stations are very close together on this section of line and the platform canopy of the next station, Durrington-on-Sea, appears to be discernible in the distance. The roof of West Worthing's three-road berthing shed (now back in commission after some years of disuse) is visible above the train, together with another '4 Vep' unit stabled on the track that connected via a headshunt to the former goods yard. This was located out of sight behind the shed and locomotives had to reverse to gain access, so shunting here was always a tricky operation. The author well remembers immaculate LBSCR K Class 'Mogul' steam engines shunting the yard. The track in the right foreground served a bay platform that, in recent times at least, has only been used for berthing defective stock. *Author*

4 Vep

The distinctive and unmistakable portal of Bincombe South tunnel (56 yards long) provides an immediate clue to the location of this illustration, which was a favourite haunt of many photographers in steam days. This picture shows '4 Vep' unit No.3005 (not to be confused with the '4 Rep' of the same number!) dashing down the 1 in 52 gradient towards Weymouth with an unidentified train which had apparently originated at Waterloo. This shot was taken on 21st May 1988, just five days after the inauguration of timetabled electric working, so the sight of one of these units in the Weymouth area at that time was quite novel. This unit sports the early version of Network SouthEast livery with the angled upsweep at the unit ends which was later altered to a curve. This unit was damaged in the Clapham Junction collision of December 1988 and was 'facelifted' during repairs, emerging as No.3405. The untidy pile of rubble in the foreground is probably the remains of Upwey Wishing Well Halt which was closed from 7th January 1957. *Colin Caddy*

4 Vep

A Charing Cross to Margate train, with '4 Vep' unit No.3543 leading, rushes down the 1 in 143 gradient at Polhill, between Knockholt and Dunton Green, on 26th August 1994. The train has just emerged from Polhill tunnel which takes the line underneath the North Downs. The unit seen here was one of the last batch of forty-one '4 Veps' constructed in 1973/74 and it entered service as No.7873, later becoming 3173. Upon 'facelifting' it became No.3543, but it should be noted that '4 Vep' units receiving this enhancement exchanged motor coaches with other units, No.3543's MSB being previously formed in No.7717, a much earlier unit built in 1967. The reason for this exchange of MSBs was because they required extensive work to convert part of the guard's brake van into passenger accommodation which meant that the MSBs were in works for longer periods than the other coaches. It was better from the stock availability viewpoint to exchange the MSBs, rather than have a unit out of traffic unnecessarily simply waiting for its motor coach to be released from repair. This unit was withdrawn in November 2004 and scrapped in South Wales during the following month. *Ken Smith*

Unlike the '4 Cig' units, very few '4 Vep's were painted in all-over white livery prior to receiving Connex colours, and the nine units that did appear in this livery did not last long in this condition. Here, unit No.3541 forms the rear portion of the 10.02am Victoria to Portsmouth Harbour/Bognor Regis train which was photographed passing Salfords on 28th February 1997. The front unit is '4 Cig' No.1753 which has recently been purchased for private preservation by Mr Neil Bird who, like the author, is a resident of Burgess Hill. Many enthusiasts no doubt contemplate buying their favourite locomotive or item of rolling stock, but few have the determination or commitment to embark on such an undertaking, let alone actually seeing it through to completion. What an achievement! No.1753 is now stored on a private site in East Anglia. The former goods yard at Salfords was used as a stone terminal for some years, hence the wagons on the right of the shot. *Colin Price*

The interior of '4 Vep' TSO No.71027 (unit No.3498) is depicted in this illustration taken at Charing Cross on 18th July 2002: these vehicles had 98 seats for second class passengers. These units can hardly be described as the most luxurious, or even comfortable, stock to travel upon with their five-a-side seating, very narrow aisles and lack of space for heavy luggage. In addition they could be very draughty, even if all of the windows were closed, because they had a door to each seating bay to facilitate quick loading at stations. But at least they could convey huge numbers of passengers and were ideal for moving vast crowds at the height of the rush hour. *Colin Scott-Morton*

Icy weather has always caused trouble for the railway operating authorities in areas where power is taken from an electric conductor rail. On the former SR the third rail is unprotected, so is especially vulnerable in bad weather. In this picture, taken on 31st January 2003, the 7.48am East Grinstead to Victoria train is seen near Crowhurst with the units' pick-up shoes arcing considerably in the snowy conditions: the units are '4 Vep' Nos. 3515 and 3517. In frosty weather overnight de-icing trains run to a pre-determined itinerary to ensure that all lines have been covered prior to the start of the following day's train service. But even this cannot guarantee a problem-free rush hour because if rain falls after the third rail has been treated and then freezes, it can create an impenetrable barrier to current collection, thus creating a disastrous situation in which electric services are brought to a standstill.
Colin Scott-Morton

4 Vep

The West Coast Line from Brighton to Portsmouth is not blessed with much photographic potential, but at least the bridge over the River Arun at Ford offers reasonable opportunities for photographers. The 29th of January 2004 was a clear day of unbroken sunshine and conditions were almost perfect in the late afternoon when the 3.00pm Brighton to Basingstoke train, formed of an unidentified South West Trains '4 Vep', rumbled over the bridge. The river here is tidal, which probably accounts for the water not being quite as still for a reflection as the photographer would have wished. The workings of slam-door stock on this service came to an abrupt end with the May 2004 timetable change when modern units took over. Slam-door stock reappeared on certain services, however, from the December 2004 timetable change. The first bridge at this location, built in the 1840s, was an unusual telescopic type which carried only a single track. It was replaced in 1862 by a double track structure, also with a movable span to permit the passage of vessels. The cessation of shipping movements to Arundel allowed the old Victorian bridge to be replaced with a fixed span bridge in 1938, in time for electrification. *Author*

4 Vep

A scene at Waterloo East on 3rd March 2004, showing the 9.05am Charing Cross to Margate working awaiting departure with '4 Vep' unit No.3582 on the rear. The vehicle nearest to the camera is former '4 TC' driving trailer second No.76275, a coach with a fascinating and colourful history that outlived similar vehicles by more than ten years and, by the date of this picture, was reputed to be the oldest carriage in general service use on the national network. It was built as Mk.1 TO (later TSO) No.3925 at Eastleigh Works in 1954 and would have been finished in carmine and cream livery which was in vogue at that time. The carriage ran on the SED in the 1950s as a 'loose' vehicle allocated to continental boat trains, and was later formed in special traffic set No.237 which was sometimes used for railtours. No.3925's interesting career as a locomotive-hauled coach came to an end in late 1965 when it was sent to York Carriage Works for conversion to No.76275 (part of unit No.404), and was destined to spend the ensuing twenty-five years on the Bournemouth Line. It finished up in '6 Rep' No.1904 which was withdrawn in February 1992, but No.76275 was transferred during the following

month to '4 Vep' No.3473 which had lost its DTC in a collision (and subsequent fire) with a car at Beltring in December 1991. In July 1992 No.76275 was involved in another reform, and this time found itself formed in No.3169 where it remained. In February 1995 No.3169 was sent to Eastleigh Works for a 'facelift' and emerged as No.3582. Coach No.76275 received only a standard heavy repair, however, probably due to the fact that no '4 TC' vehicles ever received programmed 'facelift' treatment and, therefore, presumably no drawings or specification existed. Thus this coach retained its incandescent lighting and became the last former SR emu coach with this equipment. No.76275 enjoyed remarkably good fortune to survive as long as it did as the sole representative of its type and, perhaps, it was inevitable that this charmed life would come to an abrupt end. This occurred when it was involved in a minor runaway incident at Ramsgate in April 2004 and immediately withdrawn, becoming one of the first of nearly 200 '4 Vep' units to suffer this fate. *Author*

Coach No.76339 (previously part of unit No.3024) had been held as 'spare' following a collision at Copyhold Junction, near Haywards Heath, on 6th November 1985 and in March 1990 it entered Eastleigh Works to be used as a 'guinea pig' for a 'facelift', although the work actually undertaken was more drastic than this description implies. The first class compartments and toilet were removed and replaced with ordinary '4 Vep'-style saloon seating. The original sidelights and sliding ventilators (which had previously been sealed) gave way to one-piece sidelights identical to those being fitted to other units (until the funds evaporated!). In July 1992 No.76339 was formed with unit No.3473. Here this coach, which was unique, is seen at Ramsgate in January 2004. Sadly, this unit was withdrawn on 30th December 2004. *Author*

The bridge across the River Hamble at Bursledon has always been a favourite spot for photography and here an unidentified South Central '4 Vep' forming a Southampton to Victoria via Hove service crosses the bridge on a glorious 14th April 2004, a really beautiful spring day. The roadbridge, which carries the M27 motorway over the river, is partially visible in the background. This unit is one of those fitted with large sidelights in most vehicles, which replaced the smaller windows and sliding toplights. The latter were unsuccessful and were sealed out of use, as previously mentioned. The motor coach would have been formed with the three trailer vehicles during 'facelifting' and, therefore, is not the unit's original MSB which accounts for its different windows. *Author*

4 Vep

In the year 2004 slam-door units in Network SouthEast livery could still be seen working with South Eastern and South West Trains, notably '4 Cep's and '4 Cig's on the former and four '4 Vep's (or derivations thereof) on the latter. On South Central only sliding door stock is still working in NSE colours at the time of writing. So, years after NSE ceased to exist, its controversial red, white and blue rolling stock livery could still be admired or lambasted, depending on one's point of view! In this illustration '4 Vep' No.3415, still in NSE livery, leads a Waterloo to Portsmouth peak hour train away from Petersfield in April 2004. *Author*

One of the loveliest photographic locations in southern England is this comparatively little-known spot overlooking the nine-arch Eynsford viaduct, on the Swanley to Ashford line. The viaduct takes the line across the River Darent, and for the next six miles or so, as far as Otford, the railway runs along a ledge on the hillside above the unspoilt valley and offers superb views. It is difficult to believe that it is so close to London! In this picture an unidentified '4 Vep'/'4 Cig' combination crosses the viaduct in glorious evening lighting conditions with the 5.27pm Ashford International to Cannon Street train on 14th May 2004. A few hundred yards up the line from here lie some of the most interesting railway 'archaeological remains' in the former SR area. They are the remnants of two platforms constructed in the late 1930s for the proposed Lullingstone station, which was intended to be a junction with a short branch to a new airport. Some buildings and a substantial footbridge were actually built, but the scheme was deferred due to the Second World War and subsequent 'Green Belt' planning restrictions put paid to any further development. The station was never opened but, bizarrely, was advertised in Southern Railway timetables and other literature for a few years. The buildings were demolished in 1955, the platform canopies apparently finding further use at Canterbury East, where they replaced an extremely dilapidated overall roof. *Author*

4 Vep

The decision of South West Trains to repaint one of their '4 Vep' units in 1960s blue livery to commemorate the slam door stock was widely praised but, at least in the author's opinion, the result was not entirely convincing. For a start the unit, No.3417, was not, of course, in original form, its MSB (built as part of unit No.7775) having been modified to provide additional seating. Furthermore, the red tape smothering the modern railway prevented the reinstatement of its original number (7717) and also, presumably, enforced the painting of a full-width yellow warning panel on the cab fronts, which ruined any chance of giving the unit the true '1960s look'. The aluminium window frames had long since been painted over, so recourse was made to (what appeared to be) aluminium paint, which also did nothing to enhance the unit's appearance. Even when seen from a distance the unit did not look quite right, as is apparent here in this shot of No.3417 passing Chalton Down, between Rowlands Castle and Petersfield, on the rear of a northbound train in September 2004. *Author*

The 9.52am Tunbridge Wells to Horsham train, formed of '4 Vep' No.3514, approaches Gatwick Airport station on 14th January 2005. Another '4 Vep' heads northwards on the up line. The former unit first saw the light of day as No.7837 and entered traffic on the SWD on 14th October 1972. It was 'facelifted' at Eastleigh Works in April 1990 and allocated to Lovers Walk depot on release. It ran briefly in white livery in early 1997, but was finished off in full Connex colours a few months later. It was despatched to Eastleigh for a further overhaul late in 2001 and emerged on 11th December in the new South Central green livery, joining the elite band of unique units by becoming the only '4 Vep' to carry these colours. *Author*

Following trials with prototype unit No.7755 in the early 1970s, twelve '4 Vep's were modified, renumbered and became a dedicated fleet for use on the Victoria to Gatwick Airport service. The units were reclassified '4 Veg'. The units concerned were Nos.7788 to 7799 which became Nos.7901 to 7912: the first unit to be released following modification was reportedly No.7902 on 3rd May 1978. Extra luggage space was provided by removing a number of second class seats which resulted in the seating capacity being reduced to 208 compared to 232 in a standard unit. Two racks were located at the end of each DTC adjacent to the driver's door, displacing four seats, and also in the other second class vehicles, displacing eight seats in each. The units received exterior identification vinyls at cantrail level, initially with a red (or yellow for first class) background, but later in green. These units retained their curtains in the second class accommodation long after they had been removed from the rest of the fleet as an economy measure. Here, unit No.7909, with the later style of vinyl and branding, leaves Redhill at the front of the 12.36pm Bognor Regis to Victoria train on 22nd May 1979. One wonders how visitors from Rapid City, South Dakota, U.S.A. would have reacted to the branding. Perhaps they may have been a trifle confused! *Chris Evans*

Electrification of the Bournemouth Line, the last steam-worked main line in Great Britain, was one of the first major schemes for the improvement of the network approved during the Beeching era. It was authorised at a time when closures and economies seemed to be more acceptable than investment in the railway system, and the electrification scheme was undertaken at minimum cost. Immediately the new service commenced in July 1967 it was clear that, although the 'new' stock performed well, there was insufficient rolling stock in reserve in the event of a failure and the SR struggled to maintain the advertised service. When programmed running gear overhauls on the '4 Rep's commenced this would have reduced the number of available units further, so it was decided to form-up an 8-car unit from '4 Vep' vehicles, which was christened '8 Vab'. This was made up of three motor coaches, four driving trailers and a locomotive-hauled restaurant buffet car which was adapted for use with electric stock, so it was an exceptionally powerful train. Unit Nos.7739, 7741 and 7742 were disbanded to form the new unit, which entered traffic in April 1968, and the catering vehicle was No.1759. The latter had its heating system modified to make it compatible with electric stock, had its side buffers removed and was fitted with fixed-head buckeye couplings rather than the drop-head variety fitted to locomotive-hauled stock. The motor coaches were formed with the brake van end adjacent to the first class section in the driving trailer vehicles, this being the reverse of normal practice. Another curious feature of this unit was the proliferation of electric current pick-up shoes because, in addition to shoes on the driving trailer coaches, each motor coach was also fitted with a shoe, giving seven on each side. The '8 Vab' was restricted to semi-fast services that did not involve a Weymouth portion. The unit could work with another '4 Vep', but, contrary to popular belief, was unable to work in multiple with a '4 TC' unit, which it would have been unable to light or heat. The creation of this unit certainly got the SR management of the day out of a predicament. From June 1971 the unit was only officially diagrammed on summer Saturdays, but in reality was normally used on about three days per week, usually making two return trips daily between Bournemouth and Waterloo. The unit lasted much longer than anybody had ever intended and was not disbanded until early 1975, by which time a further four '4 Rep' units had been built. The extensive alterations carried out on the buffet vehicle rendered it unsuitable for further use as a locomotive-hauled coach and it was scrapped in 1977. Here, the '8 Vab' is seen at Surbiton on 1st October 1970, with a '4 Vep' on the rear. The front three coaches were built as part of unit No.7741. The coach in blue/grey livery is the buffet car. *Bryan Rayner*

During the first months of electric traction on the Bournemouth Line in 1967 the SR struggled, as previously mentioned, to maintain the advertised service due to a chronic lack of resources. The '8 Vab' unit was hastily put together to relieve the situation. Twenty years later, when the replacement of the '4 Rep'/'4 TC' fleet was being planned, it was decided to use the original '4 Rep' 546-type traction motors in the new stock. This meant that a number of the latter units had to be taken out of traffic in rotation, so the motors could be removed for overhaul and fitting to the new units prior to them entering traffic. Once again, this would have left the operating authorities short of stock to run the timetabled service, so it really was a case of history repeating itself! Desperate measures were taken to keep the advertised service running and a multitude of *ad hoc* formations were seen, including double-headed class 73s on some trains and '4 TC' units running as five-car sets formed with a '4 Rep' buffet car. Perhaps the most interesting development was the creation of six '3 Rep' units (Nos. 2901 to 2906) which were formed of a '4 Rep' motor coach, buffet car, trailer brake first and a class 73 locomotive in place of the second motor coach. The motor coaches used for these units were previously formed in Nos. 2001/3/7, which had been stripped of blue asbestos, whilst most trailer vehicles were from '4 Rep's, previously 'spare' or came from '4 TC' stock. These remarkable permutations were no doubt of immense interest to railway aficionados, but probably caused a vastly increased workload at Bournemouth depot, not to mention numerous headaches for the operating staff. In this picture, which was taken at Eastleigh on 27th March 1988, '3 Rep' No.2903 plus No.73130 await departure with the 1.48pm Weymouth to Waterloo train. This unit, which entered traffic on 5th March 1988, was made-up entirely of vehicles from '4 Rep' No.2007, but this, and No.2902, were the exceptions, the others being formed of an assortment of coaches from various sources, as previously stated. It remained in service until 6th May 1988, so it had a very brief existence. The class 73 locomotives were usually formed on the London end of the unit, but it should be noted that no specific locomotives were allocated to these sets and they were changed over for scheduled maintenance as required at Bournemouth or Clapham Yard. *Terry Phillips*

An ideally situated block of flats has provided generations of photographers a grandstand view of train movements at Waterloo, and in this picture the 5.44pm to Bournemouth, formed of two '4 TC' units being propelled by a '4 Rep', is seen leaving on 19th June 1986. The train is running from the down Windsor slow line to the down main fast track. During the early 1960s the SR experimented with push-pull working, which was quite revolutionary at the time for main line operation, and timetabled passenger trains using this method of operation were introduced on the Oxted Line in 1966. These used a BRCW Type 3 (later Class 33) diesel locomotive and specially adapted set of former emu coaches. The trials were successful and this system was authorised by the Ministry of Transport for use on the Bournemouth Line, electrification of which had been approved in 1964. Eleven high-powered 'tractor' units, known as '4 Rep's, were to be used on the electrified section from London to Bournemouth where diesel traction would take over a portion of the train (an un-powered '4 TC' unit) for the rest of the journey to Weymouth. The '4 Rep's consisted of two motor coaches, a trailer brake first and a trailer restaurant buffet coach. The motor coaches each had four 400hp 546-type traction motors, so the 3,200hp units were very much more powerful than any of the SR's existing electric units. In order to minimise expenditure the '4 Rep'/'4 TC' vehicles were converted, mostly at York carriage works, from existing locomotive-hauled coaches, apart from the motor coaches which were new build. Despite the uninspiring and somewhat dated rolling stock provided for the route, following the inauguration of the electrification business on the Bournemouth Line boomed and justified the construction of a further four '4 Rep' units which entered traffic in 1974.
Dick Franklin

4 Rep

An evening Bournemouth to Waterloo train, powered by '4 Rep' No.2012 (formerly 3012), is depicted near Lyndhurst Road station on 24th May 1986. This was one of the later units from the small batch that entered service in 1974, thus enabling the frequency of the train service to be increased to meet growing demand. The batches were largely similar, but had a few detail differences such as the provision of lifting lugs on the first series, a design feature that was not repeated on the second batch. The buffet cars were also different. An interesting aspect of this stock was the provision of two current collection shoes on each side of the motor bogies. The unique nature of the '4 Rep' units, coupled with the special train crew knowledge, ensured that this stock rarely strayed away from the Bournemouth Line, apart from maintenance trips to Chart Leacon. They did operate over the Portsmouth Direct route on occasions due to engineering work, with locomotive haulage over the non-electrified stretch between Havant and Southampton, and also between Eastleigh and Basingstoke via Laverstock loop, again locomotive-hauled. *Bryan Rayner*

The two batches of '4 Rep' units, as previously noted, were broadly similar apart from the buffet coaches. Two different types of locomotive-hauled buffet cars were modified for use in each of the batches, those in the first series being RBs (restaurant buffet) vehicles, whilst the buffet cars in the 1974 series were rebuilt from RUs (restaurant unclassed). This was reflected in the internal layout of the converted coaches, where the arrangement of the counter and bar areas differed, but the number of seats (23) was the same. Here, the interior of buffet car No.69025 (unit No.3015) is shown and this shot was taken when it was out of service at Bournemouth depot on 10th January 1975. This coach was formerly RU No.1935 which was constructed by the Birmingham Railway Carriage & Wagon Co. Ltd. All of the cars operating on the SR were named, this being displayed on a 'pub style' sign behind the bar: No.69025 was named after a river and known as *The Stour. Chris Evans*

In 1990 the South Hampshire electrification project was completed, involving the lines from Portsmouth to Eastleigh and Southampton. No new rolling stock was authorised as part of this scheme, and the train service had to be provided from existing resources. It had been planned to retain the three '4 Rep' units that had been stripped of blue asbestos, but one of these units, No.2003, was partially written-off following the Clapham Junction disaster and this caused a change of plan. A revised scheme was formulated to make-up four '6 Rep' units, numbered 1903 to 1906, using four of the five remaining '4 Rep' motor coaches, and the 'new' stock was earmarked for use on the new Portsmouth to Waterloo via Eastleigh service. The units were formed of a motor coach, trailer brake standard, two trailer firsts, a trailer brake standard and a driving trailer standard. It should be noted, however, that one of the trailer first coaches was normally downgraded to standard class. The formation of these units involved the fitting of shoe-gear to the former '4 TC' driving trailer coach to prevent the units becoming 'gapped' on breaks in the conductor rail. In this portrait '6 Rep' No.1903, with its motor coach leading, is seen near Brookwood with a Portsmouth to Waterloo via Eastleigh working in August 1990. Perhaps it should be mentioned that unit Nos.1901 and 1902 were '4 Rep's, these units being formed of surplus '4 Rep'/'4 TC' vehicles in late 1988: they did not include a buffet vehicle. These units were disbanded in mid-1990. *Bryan Rayner*

6 Rep

Unit No.1903 is seen again, but this time berthed at Clapham Junction between duties on 27th July 1991. The composition of the unit seen here is very different to that depicted in the previous shot. By the date of this picture nearly all of the vehicles formed in the original No.1903 had either been transferred to other units or converted for departmental use. Only the motor coach, No.62145, survived of the original formation, but by this time formed intermediately and not at one end as hitherto. The revised formation of No.1903 was now driving trailer standard, trailer brake standard, trailer first (partially downgraded), motor open standard, followed by another trailer brake standard and driving trailer standard. One of the objectives of the reforming was to reduce the excessive number of first class seats, and in their new guise the units had seating for 36 first and 264 standard class passengers compared to 72 and 208 respectively in the old formation. It should be noted, however, that the ratio of first to standard class seats in the old formation was much different if the TFK was downgraded. A considerable amount of work was done to convert the motor coach, including the stripping out of the cab, panelling over of the front windows and jumper cable recesses. The cab side windows were retained, however, and the driver's entrance vestibule doors were permanently locked out of use. Shoe-gear was fitted, as required, to the bogies at the extreme ends of the units. All of the coaches still in blue/grey livery were repainted in NSE colours. During the summer of 1991 the stock regularly formed a number of mostly peak-hour trains, including the 6.00am Bournemouth to Waterloo, 7.07am Portsmouth to Waterloo via Eastleigh in the morning and 5.32pm Bournemouth and 5.56pm Poole/Portsmouth departures from Waterloo in the evening. It would be an understatement to say that these units were something of a white elephant, however, as few train crews were familiar with them and one unit was understandably 'blacked' by Waterloo station's fitters when they discovered that they had not received training on relocated equipment. Furthermore, they were none too reliable in service. Despite the financial outlay on reforming and modifying the stock the decision was taken to withdraw them at the end of the 1991 summer timetable, but actually unit Nos. 1901 and 1904 were retained for the leaf-fall season and did not finally finish working until February 1992. *Alex Dasi-Sutton*

The up 'Royal Wessex', formed of '4 TC' unit No.417 being propelled by Type 3 No.D6535, leaves Hamworthy Junction on 22nd April 1967. At this time the Bournemouth Line train service was an amazing hotchpotch of steam, diesel, electro-diesel and electric traction and the train seen here had been booked for a Class 47, hauling locomotive-hauled stock, until 3rd April 1967 when it became a Type 3/'4 TC' working. The Type 3 would have been detached at Bournemouth, the train being powered for the remainder of the journey by a '4 Rep' unit. The introduction of the new Bournemouth Line stock was heralded by the SR management of the day who stressed the additional comfort the new trains would provide. In reality, the austere style of the converted units, with largely thin, hard seating and interior appointments little better than those of pre-war trains must have disappointed passengers, who got a raw deal compared to those in other parts of country where, in total contrast, brand new, air conditioned carriages were about to come on stream. Externally the all-over 'monastic blue' livery, with an unattractive egg-shell finish, did little to enhance the appeal of the stock. *Colour-Rail*

A riot of autumn colours dominates the background of this photograph of the mid-day Reading General to Portsmouth Harbour train at Botley on Sunday 2nd November 1986. The train is comprised of '4 TC' unit No.8009, which shows signs of renumbering from 409, and Class 33 No.33105. Note the delightful vintage signal box and platform shelter plus the branch platform which was formerly used by trains to and from Bishops Waltham. The asbestos-clad structures in the background are part of a stone terminal. *Terry Phillips*

4 TC

A scene at Moreton, between Dorchester and Poole, showing '4 TC' unit No.8019 and a Class 33 locomotive forming the 10.32am Weymouth to Waterloo train on 11th April 1988. When these units were repainted in blue/grey livery with full yellow ends they became almost indistinguishable from ordinary emu stock, apart from their lack of shoe-gear and under-floor equipment. Perhaps the low level electric train heating jumper was the most obvious difference. The '4 TC' units were formed of two driving trailer second saloon coaches at the outer ends, a trailer first corridor and a trailer brake second corridor. All of the vehicles were rebuilt from existing locomotive-hauled stock, mainly at York Carriage Works. It is interesting to note that some of the Mk.1 vehicles refurbished for the Bournemouth Line were already 15 years old. One coach, No.76275, was reformed in a '4 Vep' unit in the early 1990s and survived until April 2004. *Colour-Rail*

Photographed in the splendid and unmistakable surroundings of the New Forest, the
4.46pm Poole to Waterloo train, hauled by class 73 No.73138, nears Beaulieu Road on
21st May 1988. The Bournemouth Line runs virtually from north to south at this point,
which accounts for the position of the sun in relation to the line. The train is made up of
a '5 TCB' unit, which was a '4 TC' unit with a '4 Rep' buffet car inserted as the middle
vehicle. This was yet another of the many and varied, short-lived permutations of
Bournemouth Line rolling stock that was employed in order to keep the advertised service
running together with the appropriate catering facilities. Four of these units, Nos. 2804 to
2807, were put together and it is recorded that all were in traffic from the start of the
1988 summer timetable. Two units were withdrawn when the winter timetable commenced
in September 1988, while the remainder lasted until the following May. The rear unit is
presumably a standard '4 TC'. *Chris Evans*

5 TCB

The 9.48am Bournemouth to Waterloo train, powered by class 73 No.73111, passes Worting Junction on 25th June 1988. The rear unit appears to be an ordinary '4 TC', but the leading unit is another of the oddities that typified Bournemouth Line operations in the late 1980s during the time the much-delayed Class 442 units were being introduced. It is '5 TCT' No.8101, a makeshift unit which was formed of a driving trailer standard, trailer first, trailer brake standard, trailer first and driving trailer standard. Four of the coaches had previously formed '4 TCT' unit No.8101 while a further trailer first coach came from disbanded unit No.8106. The '4 TCT' units had a first class compartment stripped out for a catering trolley, so the 'new' No.8101 ran with two first class compartments in this condition. One of the trailer first vehicles was downgraded to standard class, and in this form the unit seated 36 first and 196 standard class passengers. Both of the trailer first coaches depicted here still have yellow cantrail stripes and '1's on the doors, so presumably the downgrading was achieved by internal paper labelling only. This peculiar hybrid unit was only in traffic for a brief period, from 2nd May until 20th August 1988, so the author was pleased when this exceptionally rare picture was submitted. Judging by the flaking roof paint the vehicles were overdue for works attention, but when the unit was withdrawn they were surplus to requirements and all went for scrap.
Chris Evans

Slam door trains as they will always be remembered: in this shot a lady passenger prepares to board unit No.3417 at Waterloo. Some doors have been left open at various angles by passengers who have just alighted, whilst some droplights are up and others are down! It was so simple and straightforward, one got in, closed the door, and sat down. No messing about with silly buttons in order to open the doors! Announcements during the journey on slam door trains were often made by a gruff-voiced guard and were usually restricted to advising passengers of the train's next stopping station. On today's modern stock passengers are subjected to an incessant and irritating barrage of announcements on a variety of topics. There is no escape! On South West Trains, even passengers in the 'quiet' coach are forced to listen to the mental torture of non-stop announcements. Let us hope that the train operators don't consider piped music or advertising! *Mark Kehoe*

South West Trains was the first train operating company to eliminate the bulk of its slam door fleet and, ironically, it will also be the last company to operate these units. Two '4 Cig' units were converted to 3-car units, modified and repainted in 'heritage' liveries for use on the Brockenhurst to Lymington branch in Hampshire. Unit No.1497, in BR blue and grey livery, is named *Freshwater* whilst No.1498, in SR green livery, is named *Farringford*. The latter is seen at Lymington Town. Unfortunately, the renovation of these units was carried out with little regard to authenticity and purists were quick to point out that Phase Two '4 Cig' units never carried BR green livery nor did any unit of that type carry the raised aluminium BR 'double arrow' symbol. Southern ran its final booked slam door working on 19th August, this being the 5.17pm Victoria to Eastbourne/Seaford train. The train's departure from Victoria was preceded by repeated public announcements and a large contingent of enthusiasts was on board. Southern have, however, retained some units in reserve and some of these have been in use on mainly London to Littlehampton (and vice versa) peak-hour services on an *ad hoc* basis. South Eastern Trains still had '4 Cep' No.1698 in use at the time of writing (late August 2005) in addition to a small, but rapidly declining, fleet of '4 Vep' units. *Capital Transport*

Tailpiece